The Stone

by David P. Welden

David Welden (signature)

DORRANCE PUBLISHING CO., INC.
PITTSBURGH, PENNSYLVANIA 15222

ISBN-10: 0-8059-7009-6
ISBN-13: 978-0-8059-7009-8
Printed in the United States of America

First Printing

For information or to order additional books, please write:
Dorrance Publishing Co., Inc.
701 Smithfield Street
Third Floor
Pittsburgh, Pennsylvania 15222-3906
U.S.A.
1-800-788-7654
Or visit our website and online catalogue at
www.dorrancebookstore.com

Dedication

To Zecharia Sitchin, who more than anyone else has
made this book possible, and may it help him to acquire
the recognition he deserves.

Contents

Part One

Ufos and Abductions

Foo Fighters

The first I knew about UFOs was right after World War II. At that time the Air Force was part of the Army. The B17 and B24 pilots and crews were seeing these strange lights that would fly alongside of them and suddenly streak away at a tremendous speed or simply blink out. They called them Foo Fighters after a popular comic strip. They appeared to be remotely controlled probes for observation purposes. I never doubted that these men were telling the truth.

Behind the Flying Saucers
by Frank Scully

In 1951, I was walking by a book store in Amarillo, Texas. There in the front window was a book called *Behind the Flying Saucers* by Frank Scully. Being interested in UFOs, or flying saucers as they were called in those days, I bought the book.

The basic story started like this.

It happened on March 8, 1950. Three hundred fifty students of the University of Denver skipped lunch to hear a confidential scientific discourse delivered by what the press described later as "an unidentified middle-aged lecturer." He delivered a sensational lecture. He gave the whole inside story of a flying saucer that he said had landed within 500 miles of where he was now talking. He described the spaceship and its personnel in such detail that the undergraduates and faculty members left the lecture room with their heads spinning.

Although the story was mind-boggling, finding out who the lecturer was soon became the mystery that had to be solved first. It was recalled some hours later that the lecturer had been escorted by one George T. Koehler, a staff member of an independent Rocky Mountain radio station with the call letters of KMYR. Koehler had never introduced the lecturer by name to anybody.

Before beginning the main body of his talk, the lecturer explained that he would purposely have to leave out certain names, dates, and places, and that he must not be asked about them, as some of the scientists were working on security projects.

The lecture was arranged for students of a basic science class on the condition that it was not to be publicized. But from a group of 90 students, the gathering had grown by the grapevine to a capacity audience. However, the big question remained: who was the lecturer?

The lecture happened on March 8, 1950, but by March 17, Denver's faculty, student body, press, and Air Force Intelligence Officers were pretty well convinced they had identified the lecturer.

Four students, as well as Barron Beshoar, Denver's bureau manager of Time Life Incorporated, were sure from *Denver Post* photographers that the man was Silas Mason Newton, president of the Newton Oil Company; amateur golf champion of Colorado in 1942: graduate of Baylor University and Yale; employee of the University of Berlin, rediscoverer of the Rangely Oilfield, patron of the arts, and man of the world.

Silas Newton believed that oil deposits could be located by microwaves and he owned some super-secret microwave equipment which he used to locate oil deposits.

In the summer of 1949 Silas Newton met Dr. Gee (a fictitious name given to him by Frank Scully), a magnetic engineer who had been released in July after seven years of government servitude on all sorts of top-drawer projects. He had become a master of magnetic energy. But $7200 a year was all he could make for all his mastery, so he begged off government projects. Newton's microwave equipment would detect the location of the oil but not the volume. Dr. Gee thought a magnatron, such as had been developed during the war, might be able to detect the volume.

The First Downed Saucer

While driving with Dr. Gee from Denver to Phoenix one day early in the summer of 1949, Newton tuned in on a news commentator who happened to be reporting a flying saucer story. "Do you think there's anything to these things, Doctor?" Newton asked the magnetic research scientist.

The doctor nodded his head. "Too bad we weren't associated before," he said. "I could have worked you into the project of the first one we were called in to examine." He pointed south of where they were driving, and this is what he reported.

Two tenescopes caught an unidentified ship as it came into our atmosphere. They watched its position and estimated where it would land. Within a few hours after it landed, Air Force officers reached the flying field at Durango, Colorado, and took off in their search for the object.

When they found it, it was in a very rocky high plateau territory, east of Aztec, New Mexico. They immediately threw a guard around it. Then Dr. Gee and seven of his group of magnetic scientists were called in to examine this strange ship. When they arrived they decided that the best thing to do was not to touch it or try to get into it. They studied the ship from a distance for two days, checking with Geiger counters and other devices.

Finally, they decided that it was probably safe. The doctor said, "Nothing had transpired inside the ship to indicate that there was life therein. Apparently there was no door to what unquestionably was the cabin. The outside surface showed no marking of any sort, except for a broken porthole, which appeared on first examination to be of glass. On closer examination we found it was a good deal different from any glass in this country. Finally, we took a large pole and rammed a hole through this defect in the ship. Having done this, we looked into the interior. There we were able to count sixteen bodies that ranged in height from about 36 to 42 inches. We assumed that there must be a door of some kind, unless these people had been hermetically sealed in a pressurized cabin. So we prodded around with the pole that we had used to push through the opening made through the broken porthole, and on the opposite side from the broken porthole we hit a knob—or a double knob, to be exact. When we pushed against that double knob, a door flew open. This enabled us to get into the ship.

"We took the little bodies out and laid them on the ground. We examined them and their clothing. I remember one member of our team saying,

'That looks like the style of the 1890s.' We examined it very closely and very carefully. They were normal from every standpoint and had no appearance of being midgets. The only trouble was that their skin seemed to be charred a very dark chocolate color. We decided the charring had occurred somewhere in space and that their bodies had been burned as a result of air rushing through that broken porthole window.

"They then began the examination of the ship itself. First they decided to take complete measurements of the ship from the outside. The skin was aluminum colored.

"The ship looked like a huge saucer, and you might almost say there was a cup in it because the cabin sat in an insert in the bottom of the saucer. The overall dimensions of the ship were found to be a fraction short of 100 feet in diameter. The cabin, which was entirely round, was 18 feet across and 6 feet in height. Exactly 45 inches of the cabin was exposed above the outer rim of the saucer. The portholes were located in this area.

"On getting into the ship, their first object was to decide, if they could determine how the ship was propelled. Some of the staff suggested pushing some of the buttons on what appeared to be the instrument board. But we all agreed after some discussion that that would be the worst possible thing we could do. If the ship started, nobody would know which button to push to stop it. There were two bucket seats in the front of the instrument board and two of the little fellows were sitting there. They had fallen over, face down on the instrument board.

"It appeared that the ship must have had an automatic type of control, so that when it came into danger or when the occupants were not in a position to operate the ship, it simply settled quietly to earth."

The Second Downed Saucer

Newton asked, "How do you determine the presence of these ships? Do you stumble on them or know the moment they come into our atmosphere?"

Dr. Gee replied, "In the laboratories and also at Alamogordo and Los Alamos and at different parts of the country we have tenescope observers who spend 24 hours a day watching for evidence of objects or ships flying in the sky. Everything that comes within range of these tenescopes is noted. If it is unfamiliar and lands, the Air Force is aware of it almost immediately and if it presents problems we or other groups are consulted.

"The second one landed near a proving ground in Arizona, as opposed to the first one, which landed near a proving ground in New Mexico. When we got to the second one we found almost the same conditions as the first, except that the door was open and the sixteen dead aliens in it were not burned or browned. In fact, the medical opinion was that they had not been dead more than two or three hours. Our conclusion was that they had died in our atmosphere when the double knob of the door was opened and air rushed into their cabin, which was probably vacuumed or pressurized for their atmosphere but not ours."

He said the second one was smaller, 72 feet in diameter, but otherwise similar to the 100-foot ship.

The Third Downed Saucer

The third ship he and the staff examined landed right above Phoenix, in Paradise Valley. "We happened to be in Phoenix, so we got there in a hurry."

One of the little men was half out of the escape door, or "hatch" as the doctor called it. The little man was dead. The other little fellow (there being only a crew of two on this ship) was sitting in his seat at the control board. He also was dead. This ship was 36 feet in diameter, and the size of the cabin and all the rest of the dimensions were in the same proportions as on the other ships.

Asked if they had any sleeping quarters or toilet facilities, the doctor explained that on the 72-foot ship, there was a very ingenious device that, when they discovered how to operate it, turned out to be the sleeping quarters. Pushed back into the corner was what turned out to be a collapsible or accordion-type screen. As it was pulled out, it moved around in a half circle so that by the time it reached the wall of the circular cabin, little hammocks had dropped down from this screen or accordion-like wall and there were the sleeping quarters for these men. He said there were also toilet facilities inside the sleeping quarters. The smallest ship, however, had no such conveniences.

Dr. Gee deduced from this that they were making round trips so fast they didn't feel the need for such facilities.

Nowadays there have been many sightings all over the world of large cigar-shaped mother ships that discharge small ships, probably like the 36-foot ship.

Newton asked, "Where is the little ship?"

"We have that one in the laboratory at the present time," replied Dr. Gee. "As soon as I get your appointment through I will be authorized to let you inspect it."

In time Newton's appointment came through, but by then the ship was dismantled and reportedly shipped to Dayton, Ohio, and all comments thereafter proscribed, denied, or ignored.

There is rather conclusive evidence that there are nine alien ships at S4, an area within Area 51. Probably the three alien ships of this story are part of that nine. The Dayton story is probably typical government misinformation.

The Travis Walton Story

Chapter One
(The Happening)

Snowflake, Arizona

Mike Rodgers was twenty-eight years old and the oldest of his seven-man crew. He had been bidding these thinning contracts from the United States Forest Service for nine years. Thinning contracts involve cutting with chainsaws all of the small trees and bushes into length (called slash) in 150-yard wide strips. The slash is piled up. The Forest Service burns all piles, carefully keeping them under control, at a time when fire danger is lowest. This eliminates almost all the fuel in 150-yard-wide strips that section off nearly the entire forest. If a fire starts, it will not burn far before running into one of these fuel breaks. Mike Rodgers' latest tree thinning contract was a 48-mile trip from Snowflake to the job sight. The last 15 miles were close to impassible; there were fallen logs and boulders and water bars (water bars are humps of dirt used to prevent the road from washing out). Every day Mike and a six-man crew made this trip in his 1965 International crewcab (it had seen its better day and quite often gave trouble). On the particular day of the happening, Wednesday, November 5, 1975, they arrived on the job sight, got out, and set their chainsaws in a row on the bare ground in the road to be fueled. Because of the danger of starting a fire, it was the only safe place. After fueling they went to work.

The men running the chainsaws were Travis Walton, Allen Dalis, and John Goulette. Dwayne Smith, Kenneth Peterson, and Steve Pierce were piling behind. Mike Rodgers followed behind the men piling the slash. He made sure the piles were neat; otherwise the Forest Service would make them go back and repile them and that would ruin a contract, money-wise.

It was hard physical work and these young energetic men required large amounts of food. It was just too much to go two four-hour stretches without eating.

The first break came after two and a half hours of work. Mike shouted over the noise of the chainsaws and gave the thumbs up. They shut off their saws and the forest stillness returned. For a half an hour quiet would reign again. They charged down the hill to the truck parked in the road below and grabbed their lunches. Some of the men sat in the truck and others sat outside to eat on the thick carpet of pine needles.

Abruptly Mike would let go an intermittent blast on the horn of the International. Their half hour break was over. They topped off their gas tanks and cranked up. Later the signal came that it was time for the second break. In the mountains sundown comes early. It gets dark very quickly when the sun slips behind the trees and then out of sight behind the high ridges. After inhaling the remainder of their lunches, they donned their coats before going back to work. Only two and a half hours to go and they could head home.

The sunset had been 15 minutes earlier, but they kept cutting in the waning light. Travis checked his watch again. It was six o'clock at last! Mike was still down the hill picking up and repiling. Travis yelled and took the liberty of giving the stop-work signal. The sound of saws died.

"Time to go," Travis announced loudly. The tired men were revitalized by the prospect of quitting for the day and by their feelings of accomplishment. We had moved a pretty good distance up the strip in the eight hours of labor.

"Let's go home!" John said enthusiastically.

Allen grumbled, "It's about time."

"We really hurt 'em today, boys," Ken exclaimed.

"Hurt me, you mean!" Dwayne said, rubbing his lower back.

"One of you boys want to help me with the stuff?" Steve asked, gathering up the nearby empty gas and oil cans. John grabbed the water jug and an oil can. Travis carried the orange plastic gas can in one hand and his saw in the other and we descended the hill.

We loaded the chainsaws and gas and oil cans into the back of the truck. After arranging the gas cans so they would not tip over and leak on the bumps, Mike slammed the tailgate tightly.

"You guys have got to start doing a better job on those piles," Mike said. "That mess I fixed up back there never would have passed inspection. I know who's making those mistakes by their position on the strip. Not mentioning any names. Let's tighten up on the specifications, all right?"

Nobody said anything. He was right. If their piling failed to pass inspection, it would delay their payday until it did pass. It was in their own interest to get it right the first time.

"Let's load up, men," Mike said.

The decrepit pickup groaned on its tired old suspension as everyone piled in. There was Dwayne by the left rear door. John and Steve were in the middle and Allen was by the right rear door. In front, Travis sat by the door, Ken sat in the middle, and, of course, Mike was driving. The seven of us usually sit in the same place every day.

"Home, James," someone said in mock elegance. Mike started the old pickup and they climbed north up the ridge toward the Rim Road. It was 6:10. Barring breakdowns, we should be home before 7:30. We left the windows down so we could cool off some. We were still warm from laboring in spite of the evening air. Mike, Ken, and Travis do not smoke and prefer to inhale unadulterated air. The four in the back seat lit up as soon as we were in the truck, eager to finally be smoking after hours without a cigarette. The fresh air coming in the window was refreshing. We usually nap on the way to work every morning, but none of them ever feel drowsy on the way back to town. The rousing activity on the job gives them a keenness that stays with them all the way home.

"Why don't we all go swimming after dinner tonight," Travis suggested. Dwayne, new to Snowflake, looked doubtful, saying, "You guys are crazy; it's too damn cold for that."

"There is a heated pool in town," Travis told him. Snowflake is a small town of only 3000, but it actually has an indoor swimming pool. "That would be a good way to soak out some of the crud and tiredness I am feeling," Mike agreed.

"I'll bring a basketball," Ken volunteered. Bouncing over the thank-you-ma'ams (water bars), the truck kept bottoming out on its springs with a dull clunking sound.

The fellows started cracking jokes about the pickup.

"Peddle harder, everyone. We'll make it yet," Ken quipped.

"Hey, Mike, do you like this thing better than a pickup truck?" one of the men called from the back seat.

The continual bouncing and bobbing of the shock-absorber-less vehicle caused Travis to add, "What he has here is a rare specimen of Australian pogo truck!"

Everybody laughed.

Just then Travis's eye was caught by a light coming through the trees from the right one hundred yards ahead. He idly thought that the glow was the sun going down in the west. Then it occurred to him that the sun had set half an hour ago.

Curious, he thought it might be the light of some hunter camped there or headlights or maybe a fire. Some of the guys must have caught sight of it too because the men on the right side of the truck had fallen silent.

As we continued up the road toward the brightness, we passed into the line of sight of it for an instant. We barely got a glimpse through the branches before we rolled past the opening in the trees.

"Son of a...," Allen started.

"What the hell was that?" Travis asked. His eyes strained to make sense of the glimmers finding their way through the dense stand of trees that was blocking our vision. From Travis's open window, he could see the yellowish brilliance washing across our path onto the road another forty yards ahead. Intrigued, he was impatient to get past the rest of the pines.

"Hurry up! Drive on up there where we can see!" somebody urged.

From the driver's seat, Mike could not look up at the same angle without leaning way over. "What do you guys see?" he demanded.

Dwayne answered, "I don't know, but it looked like a plane hanging in a tree!"

Finally our growing excitement spurred Mike into what little extra speed the pickup had left. We rolled past the intervening evergreen thickets to where we could have an unobstructed view of the source of the strange radiance.

Suddenly we were electrified by the most awesome, incredible sight we had seen in our entire lives.

"Stop!" John cried out. "Stop the truck!"

As the truck skidded to a dusty halt in the rock road, Travis threw open the door for a clearer view of the dazzling sight.

"My God," Allen yelled. "It's a flying saucer!" Mike shut off the engine and we watched, spellbound.

Impaled by the sight, they were held transfixed for one long, silent moment that seemed like eternity. You could almost hear their hearts pounding. Less than thirty yards away, the metallic craft hung motionless, fifteen feet above a tangled pile of logging slash.

The golden machine was starkly outlined against the deepening blue of the clear evening sky.

The soft yellow haze of the craft dimly illuminated the immediate area with an eerie glow. Under the weird light, the encircling growth took on bizarre hues that were very different from their natural colors. The flattened disc had a shape like two gigantic pie pans placed lip to lip with a small round bowl turned down on top. Barely visible at our angle, the white dome peaked over the upper outline of the ship.

There was no motion and no sound from the craft. It almost appeared to be dead in the air. There was no one visible anywhere. Nothing stirred. The entire scene, them, the pickup, and the spectacular intruder seemed frozen for a single instant.

Ken shattered the silence. "Damnation. This is really happening!" he said in a voice fraught with awestruck fear. Travis glanced from one to another of the stricken faces of the men. Allen was hiding down low behind the door, or as Dwayne later expressed it, "he kissed his knees." Turning back to that impelling spectacle in the air, Travis was suddenly seized with the urgency to see the craft at close range. Travis was afraid the thing would fly away and he would miss the chance of a lifetime to satisfy his curiosity about it. Travis hurriedly got out of the truck and started toward the hovering ship.

The men were alarmed by his sudden action. "Travis," Allen called lowly.

"What do you think you are doing?" Mike demanded in a loud forced whisper.

Placing his feet quietly, he quickly stalked closer to the mysterious vehicle. Stepping over a low-leaning fir sapling, he carefully picked his way through the opening in the trees. He put his hands in his pockets in response to the cooler twilight air outside the truck.

After Travis had traveled about fifteen or twenty yards, the men began urging him in strained hushed shouts to return to the truck.

"Travis! Hey, Travis!" the men warned insistently.

"Get back here, man!" he heard one of the men calling in a louder voice.

Travis stopped walking for a long, hesitant moment. He paused and turned to look back at the six men staring questioningly at him from the truck.

What should I do? he asked himself. *Maybe I am being foolhardy,* he thought. *If I go back I will look a coward and I do want to get a closer look at it....that thing won't hurt me,* he told himself. *I won't get too close...but what if there is somebody inside that thing?* Finally he reassured himself with thinking, *I can always run away.* He was committed. Without replying to the guys, he resolutely turned and continued his brazen approach.

"That crazy son of a bitch!" he heard one of the men say.

I moved more slowly, cautiously covering the remaining distance in a half crouch. He straightened as he entered the dim circular halo of light softly reflecting on the ground under the craft. He was about six feet from being directly under the machine. Bathed in the yellow aura, he stared up at the unbelievably smooth, unblemished surface of the curving hull. He was filled with a tremendous sense of awe and curiosity as he pondered the incomprehensible mysteries possible within it.

Then he became aware of a barely audible sound coming from the ship. He could detect a strange blend of low and high mechanical sounds that were intermittent high piercing, beeping points overlaid on the distant, low rumbling sound of heavy machinery. The strange tones were so mixed that it was impossible to compare them to anything familiar he could remember hearing. "Travis! Get away from there!" Mike yelled to him. He shot a fleeting look at the pickup parked in the road, then turned his attention back to studying the incredible ship.

Suddenly he was startled by a powerful, thunderous swell in the volume of the vibrations from the craft. He jumped at the sound, which was similar to that of a multitude of turbine generators starting up. He saw the saucer start wobbling on its axis with a quickening motion in a pattern like the erratic spin of a slowly moving top. The same side stayed toward me and it remained hovering in approximately the same place while it wobbled. He leaped into a crouch down behind the safety of nearby logs. He expected the saucer to then streak away. It didn't.

Cringing there, he did some real fast reassessments of his situation. He resolved to waste no time getting the hell out of there! He rose up to go and was half out of his crouch when a tremendously bright, blue-green ray shot out of the bottom of the craft. He saw and heard nothing. All he felt was the numbing force of a blow that felt like a high voltage electrocution. The intense bolt made a sharp crack or popping sound. The stunning concussion of the foot-wide beam struck me full in the head and chest!

My mind sank quickly into unfeeling blackness. From the instant he felt that paralyzing blow he did not see, hear or feel anything anymore. He didn't see what hit him. His body arched backward, arms and legs outstretched, as he was lifted off the ground. He was hurled backward through the air for ten feet. His right shoulder collided with the hard rocky earth of the ridge top, landing limply spread out on the cold ground. His body lay motionless.

"It got him," Steve yelled.

Dwayne screamed, "Let's get out of here!"

"Get this son of a bitch moving!" Allen shrieked.

Mike did not need to be asked. He fumbled as he grouped for the ignition switch. His shaking fingers seized on the key and the engine roared to life. He popped the clutch and the truck lunged forward. The knobby mud and snow tires flung rocks and clouds of dirt backward as the International spun out of the clearing. Mike gunned the old truck up the rugged, boulder-strewn track.

Galvanized into action, Mike frantically turned the steering wheel one-way and then the other in navigating the tortuous road.

"Is it following us?" he yelled over his shoulder.

Nobody answered.

"Is it after us?" he shouted again.

When no reply came, he turned to see the emotionless looks of stupefied shock on the faces of his crew. Their pale faces stared straight ahead blankly. He knew then that it was entirely up to him to get them all to safety.

In reaction to what they had seen, six hardened woodsmen were reduced to mindless terror. Trying to look back, Mike sent the pickup careening off the road, crashing over bushes and small trees. He turned around to find the truck heading toward the thick trunk of a big tree. He jerked the machine back onto the track in a spray of dirt and gravel.

Mike was fearful that the saucer would continue after them in hostile pursuit. He put his head out the open window to try to see behind and was stung in the face by the sharp pine needles of a passing limb. He kept hitting boulders and other obstacles in his attempts to look behind for signs of pursuit. He was going way too fast. A passing limb slammed into the right rearview mirror, bending it useless to the side of the truck. The old International went flying through the air over the dirt ramp of a high water bar. When it landed, it smashed down destructively on its weakened springs with a terrible crash.

This crash brought Mike to his senses. If the truck broke down, they would be stranded and at the mercy of the unknown threat they were fleeing. He slowed the truck down to ten miles an hour. He was grateful to find the truck still working and apparently capable of carrying them away.

The road turned east in a tight curve to the left. He looked south back across the curve of the road and saw the startling glow of the saucer in the gathering darkness. He was very much relieved to find that their mad dash had put some distance between them.

In diverting his attention from his driving, Mike made the wrong approach to a water bar in the road. It was the largest one and unless it was approached at the correct angle, the pickup would high center and get stuck straddling the hump. Mike stopped the truck and backed up to make another run at it.

"It doesn't look like it's after us," Mike said as he shoved the gearshift into reverse. The pause broke the men out of their shocked silence and they began to jabber hysterically. Instead of continuing on over the obstacle, they sat there with the engine running. They struggled to collect themselves and to decide what to do. Everyone was yelling at once. There was nothing but a confusion of high-pitched shouting. They were all either crying, praying, or swearing. Some did all three. Steve was sobbing out a prayer, his young face streaming with tears.

Ken stammered in dismay, "I can't believe wh—what I just saw!"

Dwayne said in a wondering voice, "I've never seen a UFO before!"

"It looked like it k—k—killed him!" Allen stuttered.

Ken shook his head, saying, "That poor guy!"

Mike asked, "I saw him fall back, but what happened to him?"

Ken said, "Man, a blue ray just shot out of the bottom of that thing and hit him all over! It just seemed to engulf him!" He was totally awestruck.

"Hell! It looked like he disintegrated!" Dwayne exclaimed.

Steve said, "No, he was in one piece. I saw him hit the ground."

"I do know one thing. It sure looked like he was hit by lightning or something!" Dwayne returned. "I heard a zap—as if he touched a live wire!"

"Damn!" John swore. "It sure knocked the hell out of him!"

"It looked like a grenade exploded in front of him and just blew him back!" Ken cried.

"Hey, man, we better go back!" someone said.

Ken agreed. "He could be hurt real bad!"

"No way, man. I ain't going back there!" Steve said.

Dwayne said, "No, we better go back. He could need help!" He asked Steve, "You don't want to stay here by yourself while we go, do you?"

Steve gave him a blank stare.

Ken insisted that they should go back and Mike agreed.

Mike turned the truck around at the turnoff and said firmly, "This truck is going back. Anybody who doesn't want to come can get out right here and now and wait! We've been acting like a bunch of cowards. We're all scared, there is no denying that. But we've got to do what we should have done in the first place!"

The embarrassed men no longer protested about returning to the site. Even if any were still reluctant, they were ashamed to say so. Also, the prospect of waiting alone at the turnoff in the dark was much worse than going back.

Their courage had been reinforced by the time and distance away from the site. However, as they turned and left off the Rim Road toward the original scene, their apprehension started steadily rebuilding. They could not stop going over and over what they had seen and what the dreadful possibilities were when they returned. "What if that thing is still there?" Dwayne questioned fearfully.

"We'll be able to see it before we get there," Mike said uncertainly. "If it is still there, we'll turn around and get the hell out of there."

"What if we find Travis's dead body lying out there?" was Allen's grisly question. Nobody replied. Nobody wanted to think about the answer to that.

They rounded the curve where Mike had last seen the saucer. They saw nothing. The pickup rolled hesitantly onward. Skittishly, the men looked all about them. They became quieter and their subdued comments came less frequently.

"Get the flashlight out of the glove box there," Mike said. Dwayne handed it to him. "I think it was right along here somewhere. You guys keep your eyes pealed," Mike anxiously suggested. He drove slowly on, scanning the roadsides.

"Hold it! It was right back there!" Ken exclaimed.

Dwayne said, "Yeah! I think it was right about here! I recognize the pile of slash over there!"

Mike sent the flashlight beam stabbing out into the darkness in the direction the men indicated. He called loudly, "Travis!" They listened intensely. No answer.

Mike pulled the truck around and pointed the headlights toward the log pile above which they had seen the hovering ship. They backed up and pulled in, driving over the fir sapling leaning in the way.

Their eyes searched the area that was illuminated by the headlights. They found nothing there. No dead body was in the clearing.

"Maybe this ain't it," Ken suggested. "All these piles look alike."

"I thought it was farther down that way," Allen said, pointing north down the ridge.

"No, I remember this spot," Dwayne insisted.

"We're just going to have to get out and look around," Mike stated. "Before we do anything, who's all coming and who is staying?" he asked.

Nobody wanted to remain behind alone. The woods were very dark.

"Leave it running," Steve suggested, as they got out of the truck. They left the doors open too. No one objected to having a quick getaway, just in case.

They searched first in the security of the headlights. Everybody stayed together, huddling close behind Mike, who carried the flashlight.

The tightly knit group searched the immediate area thoroughly, foot by foot. The flashlight beam probed into the night, examining every dark space.

They searched behind every log, bush, and stump. They called out loudly, "Travis! Travis!" Except for their calls, the woods was deathly quiet.

"Look out!" Dwayne cried, jumping. Everyone looked around. "What's the matter?" they asked him anxiously.

"Oh!" he heaved a relieved sigh. "That moon up there scared the hell out of me! I caught it out the corner of my eye and I thought it was that flying saucer coming back!"

"Travis!" they called at intervals. They looked further north as Allen had suggested, but there were no more logging slash piles there.

"Maybe he ran after us when we took off!" Ken suggested. They searched for tracks in the soft powdery dust of the road. There were no tracks but those of the truck. They found no sign anywhere. "Travis!" they called again.

The longer they continued, the more worried Mike became, and the more overcome with emotion. He stumbled for a step and stood looking down, struggling to control his feelings. The loss of his friend, his guilt at driving away, and the pressure that leadership demanded of him all became too much to bear for a moment. He silently handed the flashlight over to Ken.

Ken took him by the shoulder, saying, "You all right, Mike? Take it easy, man. Come on, it's going to be okay."

After a few moments, Mike managed to regain his composure. He finally said, "Okay, you guys, we're not doing any good here. Let's go!"

They got in the truck and began the long drive back to Heber.

The memory of what they had so recently witnessed left them with a wide spectrum of strong emotional reactions.

"That ray was the brightest thing I've ever seen in my whole life!" declared Steve. "It almost blinded me for a second."

"You're never going to catch me out here in these woods again!" vowed Dwayne.

Ken kept shaking his head. "Incredible, absolutely incredible," he said, pondering out loud.

Behind their excited talking, the men were nagged by the problem they knew they would have to face. "What are we going to do now?" somebody asked.

"Let's get a bunch of people together to go out there and help us look," Dwayne suggested.

Then Ken announced the one thing they had all avoided saying: "We're going to have to tell the authorities about this."

"The cops!" Allen exclaimed. "No way, they'll think we're nuts."

"If we don't tell them and Travis can't be found, they might suspect us," Mike pointed out.

"If we tell anybody at all, they're going to think we are crazy," Steve said.

"I know!" John said, brightening. "We'll just say that Travis is lost and not say anything about the UFO."

"We'd better tell them everything and just pray that they believe us," said Ken. "We have got to stay honest all the way through this. It's the only way we're going to be believed."

Just then the pickup rounded the bend and the comforting lights of Heber came into view. That oasis of civilization was the very symbol of salvation to them at that moment. They drove down the dark, quiet street to the nearest telephone.

They parked the truck and got out. Ken picked up the receiver and dialed "0." It was he who first broke the news to the police. Ken Peterson waited nervously for an operator to answer. He glanced at his watch. It was 7:35. All five men waited tensely while Ken talked.

"Well," Allen said, as Ken stepped out of the telephone booth.

"He's coming," Ken announced.

"Who's coming?" Mike asked. "The sheriff?"

"No, Deputy Ellison," Ken replied. "He wants us to meet him up there." He pointed toward a parking lot, a block up the street by the highway.

"What did you tell him?" Mike asked impatiently.

"Nothing," Ken answered. "I mean, at the last minute I got to thinking. If I were to tell about the UFO on the phone, he might've thought it was a crazy joke or something and hung up on me." They started toward the pickup. "I just told him one of our crew members got lost," he added lamely.

While waiting at the parking lot for Deputy Ellison, they struggled to think of a way to present their incredible report. "You know," Dwayne said, "it's gonna be awful hard for him to accept. We're gonna have to expect that."

"Hell, no, he ain't gonna believe us," Allen grumbled. "The pigs never believe anything."

This derogatory term upset the other men.

"Here we are, asking them for help," Ken said to him, "and you sit here talking about them like that."

Allen ignored the comment.

"They gotta know we're telling them the truth," John insisted. "I sure don't know what the hell we're gonna do if they don't."

"Well, we're about the find out," Mike said grimly. "Here he is."

The deputy sheriff pulled into the parking lot, pulled up to the driver's side of the truck, and stopped. The big deputy stepped out and sauntered around the car, passing in front of the headlights. Mike rolled down his window as the officer stepped up. He stood five foot ten inches and looked to weigh a strong 200 pounds. He had on the brown western-style uniform that all the county sheriff's men wear. On the lapel of the coat glinted the golden star of his badge.

"Okay, what's the problem here?"

"Well," Mike began. "A friend of ours is probably lost. At least he might be lost, anyway. I mean he might be dead!"

Ellison's interest sharpened. His eyes darted from one face to the other. Steve's reddened eyes and tear-streaked face and the various pale expressions of the others made him certain of one thing. Something very serious had happened. "What do you mean, he might be dead?"

"Well, sir...." Mike groped for words. "Its kinda hard to explain. You may think we're...I mean...I don't really know where to start!"

"How about starting at the beginning," was Ellison's impatient urging.

Ken came to Mike's rescue. He started in relating what had happened. It was like a leak springing in a dam. The others joined in, adding more information and agreeing with Ken's description. The heavy emotional impact of their recent experiences was fresh in everyone's speech. Their voices broke with emotion at the recall of their ordeal. Emotions overflowed at the first opportunity to tell someone who had not seen what they had seen. The words just poured out.

The deputy exhibited exceptional cool and reserve. He did not interrupt the men the first time through the account, except for an occasional "uh-huh" at the proper places. For a small town cop hearing such an incredible story, his composure was admirable. However, the more the men talked, the more his attitude seemed to change. Finally when they finished, Ken confronted the officer. "You don't believe us, do you?"

The surprised Ellison replied, "No, I wouldn't say I don't believe you. Though you have to admit it sounds pretty wild."

The men were relieved that the deputy was taking them seriously, but that was only part of the source of their distress. Travis's fate was the prime concern.

The deputy continued, "No, I believe you enough to where I'm going to call in and get some deputies out here to look for this man. I want some of you to come up on the hill with me. I have to radio into the central office in Holbrook. Yes, you three," he said, nodding at Mike, Ken, and Allen, the more vocal half of the group. "The rest of you stay here," he ordered.

The three got in the police car with Ellison and road to the top of the hill. The radio did not have the power to transmit out of the canyon that Heber is hidden in. Up on the hill he had a straighter shot at Holbrook, the county seat. Ellison radioed the dispatcher. He was informed that the sheriff was not in the office, but that he would radio back.

Finally Sheriff Marlin Gillespie came on the radio. Ellison explained to him that he had a missing person report involving a UFO. He briefly related what he'd been told.

Gillespie said he would come there immediately.

Ellison explained to him there would be bad road conditions. Sheriff Gillespie said that he and Undersheriff Ken Copland would bring the sheriff department's four-wheel drive pickup.

Deputy Ellison drove the three men back to the parking lot where the other three men had remained. They waited for Sheriff Gillespie to travel the forty-five miles from Holbrook.

An hour later, Sheriff Gillespie and his second-in-command, Undersheriff Ken Copland, arrived in the county's four-wheel drive pickup. Sheriff Gillespie approached Mike's window. The well-seasoned sheriff's eighteen years in law enforcement had left little to be surprised about, but here was a new one.

"Tell me again who is this fellow who is missing?" He was informed the man was Travis Walton, one of the men they worked with. "Well, let's hear it from the start. What happened?"

The lawman listened carefully while the men explained.

"It's colder than hell out here," he said. "Mind if I get in there a minute while I ask you a few questions?" He sat in the right front seat. He continued to question the men intently.

Finally he shook his head and said, "You know, this whole thing sounds crazy, but I have got to admit I'm inclined to believe you."

Faith was restored for the crewmen. They were now sure that they had done the right thing in telling the truth and reporting their problem.

The existence of UFOs was not so unheard of to the lawman. He related to them an experience he had had years ago in the same county. The men were amazed to learn that Sheriff Marlin Gillespie himself had had a close encounter with a large glowing object!

"Okay, we've got to go out and see if we can find this guy," the sheriff said. "If this fellow is hurt, we need to find him as soon as possible."

"Ain't going back out there!" Steve declared emphatically. "No way." He was filled with dread at the prospect. John and Dwayne were equally firm in their resolution not to return to what might have become a very dangerous area.

"At least some of you are going to have to come along," Gillespie said.

Ken, Allen, and Mike agreed to accompany the lawmen back to the sight of the encounter. Mike gave John permission to drive Steve and Dwayne home to Snowflake in the crew truck.

The three remaining men got into Deputy Ellison's car. Ken got in front and Allen and Mike climbed in the rear. The car was designed for streets and highways, so the fifteen miles of rough roads were a little too much for it. In driving up the last steep hill before reaching the Rim Road, the muffler fell completely off the car. Ellison got out and put the muffler in the back of the pickup. The car roared noisily on up the hill with the truck still behind.

When they reached the turnoff from the Rim Road to the contract, Ellison's car could go no further. The thank-you-ma'ams were too high for its low ground clearance. Ellison, Allen, and Ken then climbed into the paddy-wagon-style camper on the back of the pickup.

Mike rode in the front seat of the pickup with Sheriff Gillespie and Ken Copland. It was pitch dark. Gillespie shined the powerful beam of the truck's spotlight to the side of the road as they drove.

As they neared the abduction sight, everyone, including the officers, could not help feeling a bit uneasy. No one spoke. Only the sound of the engine and the tires scattering rocks could be heard as they broke into the clearing.

Mike said softly, "This is the place." The truck rolled to a stop. Copland sent the spotlight scanning back and forth around the empty clearing. They slowly got out and stood in a circle in front of the headlights.

They looked around with apprehension at the dark surrounding trees. With the temperature steadily lowering, they all hoped they would find something soon. "Ellison, you and Rodgers take the truck on the roads down below," the sheriff ordered. "The rest of us will use the flashlights and look around here."

For another endless bitter cold hour, both parties continued to search without success. Not a single trace was found of Travis, the missing man. The two groups gathered back at the clearing to exchange the bad news.

"I think we've done about all we can do here tonight," Gillespie announced. "We can only cover so much ground in the dark with the number of men we have," the sheriff continued. "I'm going to get more men out here first thing in the morning and we'll blanket the whole area. Right now we need to notify Walton's family. Who is the next of kin?"

"His mother, Mary Kellett," Mike replied. "She's staying in a cabin over east of Overgard. Bear Springs is the place."

"Okay," Gillespie said. "You go with Copland in the truck and notify Walton's mother. Ellison and I will take Dalis and Peterson back to Snowflake."

During the half hour drive, Copland remarked, "This whole thing sounds crazy as hell! If I hadn't known Ken Peterson for so long, I'd have a heck of a time believing the rest of you." He explained that he had gone to school with Ken Peterson's father and had known the family for years. "Ken just would not lie about something like this."

At this point in the story, I am going to skip the notification of Travis Walton's mother.

The Manhunt the Next Morning

The first daylight search started on November 8.

Sheriff Gillespie had managed a brief rest, but he rose early to motivate his forces. By sunrise the Navajo County Search and Rescue Team had been alerted and the Heber Forest Service recruited.

Mike's crew met at Mike's house, except for Steve Pierce. He was still in a mild state of shock. Steve did not return to those woods ever again. And for right now, he even refused to leave the house. Travis's brothers Don and Duane and his mother were also going to go to the search area. Don was very suspicious of Mike and his crew; he was sure that they had murdered Travis.

The caravan from Snowflake left for Heber. When they arrived at Heber, the sheriff's posse, U.S. Forest Service men, and the Navajo County Search and Rescue Team were gathered in front of the gas station. Police cars and four-wheel drive and green government pickup trucks crowded the big parking lot. All in all, over fifty men were present.

They drove out to the woods. Sheriff Marlin Gillespie called the men together for a briefing.

"Okay, attention everyone, gather around here. What we are looking for is a man down, or wandering around dazed, possibly injured. The man is about six feet in height, one hundred sixty-five pounds, red hair. He was last seen wearing Levi's and a blue denim jacket. If you should find anything at all, report back to me immediately. We're going to start up there at the Rim Road. We'll space ourselves out equally, staying within close sight of the man on either side at all times. When we get down to the lower road, we'll regroup and make another sweep. All right, men, let's go."

Later on that morning, a Forest Service man walked up and grabbed Dwayne Smith's shirt front and twisted it, pulling up close to his face. He said, "All right, where'd ya hide the body?"

Dwayne protested, "What body? We didn't kill anybody. Dammit, there was a flying saucer here, just like we told you!"

Travis's brother Duane walked up behind the burly Forest Ranger and said, "Hey, you. Knock it off!" The man released his grip on Dwayne Smith's shirt and turned around defiantly.

"You've got better things to do than stand around hassling people," Duane told him. The man started to speak. Then looking Duane up and down, he changed his mind. He turned and stalked off.

"We did not kill him," Dwayne Smith hotly denied. "I'll even take a lie detector test to prove it!"

"Yeah, we'll take a lie detector test, truth serum, or any damn thing they want to throw at us, 'cause we're telling the truth," John joined in. The other crew members added their agreements.

Up and down the ridges the searching sweeps went on. The search spread wider and still there was no trace of anything to raise hopes. As the afternoon dragged past, someone brought a huge load of lunches out to the weary men. Footsore groups of searchers would stop by the clearing and rest their backs against a tree while they ate.

The day was finally over and no one had found a trace of anything. When the sheriff dismissed the searchers for the day, they left under the cloud of a single, grim thought: If they found the man when the search resumed the next day, they would not find him alive. No one could survive two nights in those woods at near zero temperatures.

The second day of the search was much like the first. Sweep after sweep was made over the same search ground. The only difference was a decline of enthusiasm in the searchers. They had not found anything the day before, which only increased chances that the second would be the same. That evening, when there was still no sign, they officially called the search off.

That evening after they returned to town, Deputy Glen Flake paid Mike a visit.

"Heard you men volunteered for a lie detector test," he began. "Is everyone still willing?"

"Yeah," Mike answered. "We're willing to take any test they want to give us. We'd like to prove that what some people are saying just is not true!"

"Well, the sheriff heard that you guys were willing and he's going to take you up on it," the deputy continued. "He's arranged to give all you guys lie detector tests."

"Good!" Mike replied. "When are they going to be?"

"Eight o'clock Monday morning. You are supposed to show up at the courthouse in Holbrook," he said, getting up to leave. "Make sure nobody leaves town, all right?"

"Sure, nobody's planning to go anywhere as far as I know, but I'll tell them," Mike assured the officer as he left. Now they had a chance to prove they were telling the truth.

November 10, the day of the lie detector test. The crewmen were eager to prove that they had not murdered Travis and that they had witnessed the abduction of their coworker by a UFO.

When the men arrived at the county courthouse in Holbrook they were immediately thronged by newsmen. There were crowds of newspaper and magazine reporters, plus radio and television crews. The media men shoved microphones into the men's faces, and cameras followed them all the way into the courthouse. Some persistent newsmen took up a day-long watch outside the sheriff's office building.

After waiting 25 minutes, the men began to fidget.

Having standing-room-only conditions was aggravating an already emotionally loaded situation. Newsmen kept trying to shoulder into the overcrowded room.

"Hey, are you guys the ones who think they saw the little green men?" one of the newsmen asked sarcastically.

"Stick it!" someone called in return.

"Hey!" one of the men called to the deputy at the desk.

"How long are we going to have to stand here?"

Just then, Sheriff Marlin Gillespie entered the office. "Good morning," he said. "I've been talking things over with the polygraph examiner. He's setting up his equipment in one of the back offices we'll be using for a testing room. You guys can come with me now." He led the men back down the hallway and out into the sunshine at the rear of the building. The sheriff and a deputy led the group through a courtyard to a jail kitchen.

The six crewmen, Duane Walton, Sheriff Gillespie, and his deputy jammed the kitchen. Seating themselves on tables and benches, they waited to hear what was to happen next.

The sheriff spoke first. "I felt we needed to have a conference before we begin to let you know how the testing is going to be arranged. We've got certain rules you are going to have to follow. We can only take one person at a time. We want you all to remain back here and, as each one of you is tested, you are to remain here. However, we don't want the tested people associating with the untested people. So when you're finished, stick around. But don't converse with the untested people. These tests are going to take all day so...."

Gillespie continued, "We're going to require you to sign a consent-waiver form before testing. This statement gives us the right to test you and to use the results as evidence in a court of law. Just be sure you understand that when you sign."

Just then the polygraph examiner entered the room. "This is Mr. Cy Gilson," the sheriff introduction. "He's the Department of Public Safety polygraph examiner. He'll be the one testing all of you."

Allen spoke the thought that had been making them all uneasy: "How do we know we can trust this guy? We've heard that the government is always trying to hush these kind of things up. How do we know you're not going to rig these lie detector tests?"

Mr. Gilson snorted at the affront. "I'll guarantee you one thing. If you guys are telling the truth, those charts will show it. And if you are lying, I'll find that out too."

"Your guarantee doesn't necessarily mean anything," Mike countered. "You would say that even if you've been bought off!"

Gilson was indignant. "What's your problem?" he shot back. "Are you lying?"

"Hell, no, we're not lying!" Mike returned. "We're really only worried that you've been bought off. It's not impossible, you know. The government tries to keep these UFO things quiet."

"All right," Gillespie broke in. "HOLD ON, HOLD ON, EVERY-BODY!" His words were almost as effective as a bullet fired in the air. The men respected Sheriff Gillespie because of his fair treatment of them in the woods and the way he had handled the search. Everybody stopped talking and listened.

"Let's just calm down a minute here. You six men all calm down here. You decided to take these lie detector tests voluntarily, and if you decide not to take them, no one can stop you. But I would like to point something out to you. A lot of people are thinking that you guys are guilty of murdering Walton. You haven't been arrested yet, but things could get pretty hard for you if Walton never turns up, even if you're telling the truth. If you are telling the truth, then these tests are going to clear you. You don't have a thing to worry about from Mr. Gilson. I will give my personal guarantee that these tests will be conducted fairly."

Mike said, "What do you guys think?"

The approving looks exchanged their unspoken feelings.

"Okay, sir, if we have your guarantee, we will go on and take the test," Mike said to the sheriff.

The men drew straws to determine who would go in what order. Steve Pierce was first.

Cy Gilson went over the polygraph machine and the procedure. Gilson sat Steve down in a chair and wired him up.

When Steve coughed or moved, the needles on the machine scratched wildly back and forth on the rolling chart of paper on the machine. The tiniest fluctuation in his body responses would be precisely recorded for the examiner's expert analysis.

Steve's test lasted nearly two hours. At that rate, it was going to be a long day.

Allen Dalis's test was second. After a little over an hour, Allen came storming out of the testing room and slammed the door behind him.

"I know that son of a bitch has been bought off!" he told the waiting men. "He keeps acting like he thinks I killed Travis. I'm damned sure not lying and if the bastard says I am, then I know he is the one who's lying."

"What makes you think he's been paid off, Allen?" Mike asked him. "Did he tell you the results of the test?"

"No, it's just that he keeps acting like he don't believe us about the UFO!" Allen fumed.

"Hold on," Mike said. "There is no call to fly off the handle!" Mike, who had drawn the straw for fifth place, told them, "I will be going next and I'll have a talk with the guy. Maybe I can find out what is going on."

Mike went into the testing room and had a long talk with the examiner. He explained Allen's behavior as simply being his character and that Allen was still overwrought from seeing the UFO. Mike was then strapped to the polygraph machine's sensitive pickups and his test began. An hour and a half later, when the examiner was through, he made no comment. While he was being released from the polygraph machine, Mike said, "I told you I was telling the truth." The poker-faced Gilson still would not make any statement as to what he thought the charts showed. Mike, who had confided in the examiner and knew the truth, did not need to be told.

He went outside into the dirt courtyard and told the men that everything was all right and to go on with the testing. Ken Peterson, Dwayne Smith, and John Goulette each took their tests in turn.

Finally, John Goulette came out. Testing was over at last. It had been a long thirteen hours for everyone.

All the other men waited in the kitchen area while Travis's brother Duane and Mike went into the courthouse to find out what Gilson had to say.

Darkness had fallen and the swarm of reporters had long since drifted away. They entered the testing room and found Cy Gilson carefully putting away his polygraph instruments.

"Well, what's the final verdict?" Duane asked. The examiner seemed awed, or at least perplexed.

"I can't really say right now," he said quietly. "You will have to wait until I make my final report." Mr. Gilson said, "Excuse me a minute. I have to go wash the ink out of the pens before they dry." Duane and Mike followed him to the washroom.

"We have a right to know the results of these tests," Duane began earnestly. "When is your report going to come out?"

Gilson said, "I have to go over these charts very closely first. That should only take a few days. I will probably send the sheriff my report by the end of the week."

"Couldn't you at least tell us unofficially?" Mike persisted. "You must have some idea of how they turned out."

Examiner Gilson stopped and looked at Duane and Mike. "I guess it wouldn't hurt anything to tell you, seeing the way the tests apparently came out. So keep this under your hat and don't tell any newsmen until after I make my official report," he said. "From what I have been able to see from these charts, you men are apparently telling the truth!"

"Well, we would like to apologize for this morning," Mike said, offering his hand. "Looks like we badly misjudged you."

Gilson replied, "When I started testing you this morning, I really expected to find that a murder had been committed. After all those hard words early this morning and the way Allen Dalis reacted, I was even more sure of foul play. But none of the tests except Allen's showed anything like that. Allen was just too agitated to be tested at all. Even his charts were readable and showed foul play. He couldn't have committed a crime and made up a story about a UFO without involving five other men whose tests corroborated the report."

Cy Gilson shook his head soberly. He put his hands on the stack of lie detector charts. "Incredible," he muttered.

Chapter 2
The Return

I regained consciousness lying on my stomach with my head across my right arm. Cold air brought me awake. As I raised my head up, a white light caught my eye just before it blinked off. Either a light had been turned off or a hatch closed, which cut off the light from inside. I only caught a glimpse as I raised my head and could not be sure which it was.

Then I saw only the mirrored outline of a rounded, silvery disc hovering four feet above the paved surface of the road. It must have been about forty feet in diameter because it extended several feet off the left side of the road. It was too large for the highway and it hung off the left side because on the right side was a cutaway rock embankment. It looked to be about fourteen feet high in the center.

For an instant it floated silently above the road only a little more than a dozen yards away. I could see the night sky surrounding the trees and the highway center line reflected in the smooth unblemished hull. I noticed the faint feel of heat on my face.

Then, abruptly, it shot vertically into the sky, creating a strong breeze that stirred by nearby pine boughs and the dry oak leaves that lay in the dry grass beside the road. No light was emitted from the craft and it was almost instantly lost from sight.

The most striking thing about its departure was its quietness. It seemed impossible that something moving through the atmosphere at that speed would not have shrieked through the air or broken the sound barrier with a sonic boom. Yet it was totally silent.

I scrambled to my feet. My legs felt rubbery. I swayed, then caught my balance.

I noticed the bluish-white glowing dot of a couple of street lights down the hill. I looked around and recognized the deserted stretch of curving road as being the highway that winds down the canyon into Heber from the west. I was overjoyed to be in familiar surroundings. It felt so good to have my feet back on the sweet earth. I still felt a little pain in my head and chest, and I felt a little weak. But otherwise I was physically intact. The memory of what had happened to me ran through my mind like a reoccurring nightmare. Pondering the thought that this had really happened left me in a dazed state of shock.

I ran wildly down the deserted highway, across the bridge to Heber, stopping at the new building across from a service station. There was smoke coming out of the chimney and lights on inside, but no one answered my desperate knocking. There were no cars passing by.

I ran on down the highway, over the second bridge to the row of telephone booths at the Enco Station. I entered the first of the phone booths I came to and frantically dialed the operator. (A dime was not required at that time.) My panic was increased by the discovery that the telephone was out of order! Nearly exhausted from my wild run, I staggered out of that phone booth and into another, relieved this one was working. I dialed the operator and panted out the number of my brother-in-law, Grant Neff. He was the only nearby relative with a telephone.

Grant answered. It was 12:05 A.M. "They brought me back," I babbled. "I'm out here in Heber. Please get somebody to come and get me." My hand shook as I held the cold receiver.

Grant was not amused by the prank calls the family had been receiving. He took this call to be another cruel joke. "Uh, I think you have the wrong number," he replied sarcastically as he started to hang up.

"Wait! It's me, Travis!" I screamed hysterically into the receiver.

"Where are you?" he asked, still suspicious of a joke.

"I'm at the Enco Station."

"Okay," he replied almost apologetically, yet still cautious of a prank. "Stay right there. I'll get Don or Duane and come. You just hang on."

I remember hanging up and slumping down, cradling my head and my knees. I hugged my shins. My nerves were frayed and I was cold and weary. I waited nearly an hour for help to arrive.

Grant drove the three miles from Taylor over to Snowflake and found Duane at mom's house. He told about the call and that he had some doubts it was really me. Duane, too, thought it might be another stupid joke, but they decided they could not risk not investigating.

The rest of the family was overjoyed, but Grant and Duane cautioned them not to get their hopes up too high.

Since they were not sure, they did not notify the authorities but immediately set out for Heber, thirty-three miles away.

Lights suddenly shone in the phone booth. Relief flooded over me when I raised my head and saw it was the headlights from Duane's pick-up. Duane and Grant got out and came to where I was still slumped in the phone booth. Duane opened the glass door of the booth and helped me to my feet.

"Easy, Travis, take it easy, man!" Duane said as I tried to speak. "Don't try to talk now."

"Am I ever glad to see you!" Grant said. Duane helped me into the warm truck and asked Grant to drive. On the way to Snowflake I tried to tell them about what happened to me but I just couldn't get it out.

"They were awful. White skin....great big eyes...," I sobbed in horror.

"Take it easy. You're all right now. They didn't harm you, did they?"

"No...but those eyes, those horrible eyes! They just kept looking at me!" I choked out in broken gasps.

"Just so you're okay, that's all that counts," Duane said. "Everyone has been worried sick about you."

"If it's already after midnight, I must have been unconscious for a couple of hours," I replied shakily. "Because I only remember about an hour and a half inside that thing."

Duane and Grant looked at me strangely.

"Travis, feel your face," Duane said.

I did. "Good hell, I just shaved this morning and it feels like a week's growth!" I exclaimed, still not comprehending.

"Travis," Duane said gently, "you have been missing for five days!"

My mouth dropped open. I took a hard look at my watch. The date said 11. "FIVE DAYS," I screeched. "Good God! What has happened to me?" I ran my hand over my heavy growth of rough stubble on my jaw. "Five days?" I repeated numbly, "Five days."

My mind reeled, trying to comprehend the staggering implications of this revelation. Dazed, I started in wonder, "That means that...oh, no... that can't be...."

"As long as you are all right, there's no need to talk. Just try to calm down for right now," Duane said. To Grant he said, "That crazy mob of reporters is not going to get a hold of this guy, I'll guarantee you that right now! He's not in any shape to be talking to anyone."

Chapter 3
The Alien Ship and Occupants

What's the matter with my eyes? I asked myself. *The ceiling is all crooked. It is too small on this end and too large on that end! Tricks on my eyes?* I closed them, but opened them again. The odd-shaped ceiling was indeed as I had perceived it.

"What a weird place!" I reflected. I had no idea where I was. I could hear the sounds of movement in the room. A quiet shuffling that sounded vague and distant.

I tried to think. Something had happened and I had been hurt. Yeah, that was it...but what? I could remember straightening up and feeling as though somebody had whacked me with a baseball bat.

Suddenly, the memory of what happened before I blacked out came rushing back with stunning impact. I remember standing in a clearing in the woods looking up at that glowing saucer! Good grief, what a sight! I had seen it move and heard its awesome sound. My approach had seemed to cause the thing to come alive.

Then I recalled having stood up and turned to get away from it. I had been hurt somehow—maybe that thing had hit me with something!

Where the hell am I? Oh, my God, the hospital! I thought.

It was very hot and humid. The heavy air was almost stifling. I was sweating; warm moisture beaded my temple. Feeling my jacket bunched up under my arm, I wondered why the nurse had not removed it. I had all my work cloths on, even my boots. The jacket was just too warm. *I must be injured so bad there wasn't time to take off my coat.*

I had never been in a bad accident or hurt myself seriously. I had been pretty healthy throughout my life. I had not taken so much as a single aspirin in years. But here I had really done something stupid and it was too late to reconsider. Why in hell did I have to get so close? That was dumb.

I looked again at the reassuring forms of the doctors around me. Abruptly my vision cleared. The sudden horror of what I saw rocked me with the realization that I was definitely not in a hospital.

I was looking squarely into the face of a horrible creature!

Suddenly it clicked, the weird-shaped room. "Good God! I must be inside that craft!"

A creature was looking steadily back at me with huge, luminous brown eyes that were the size of quarters! I recoiled at the sight.

I looked frantically around me. There were three of them! I struck out at two on my right, hitting one with the back of my arm and knocking it into the other one. My swing was more of a push than a blow; I was so weak.

The one I touched felt soft through the cloth of its garment. The muscles of its puny physique yielded with a sponginess that was more like fat than muscle. The creature was light and had fallen back easily.

I got myself to a sitting position. I lunged unsteadily to my feet and staggered back. I fell against a utensil-arrayed bench that followed the curve of the wall.

My arm sent some of the instruments clattering against the back of the shelf. I leaned heavily there, keeping my eyes on those horrid creatures.

My actions caused the device on my chest to crash to the floor. The device rocked back and forth on its side. The rocking sent shifting beams of colored light on the floor. Greenish rays came from underneath the overturned instrument.

My leg felt too weak to hold me up. I leaned on the counter. The trio of humanoids started toward me. Their hands reached out toward me.

With the superhuman strength of a cornered animal, I ground out the strength to defend myself. I grabbed something from the bench with which to fend them off. My hand was on a thin transparent cylinder about eighteen inches long. It was too light to be an effective club. I needed something sharp and I tried to break the tip off the tube. I smashed the end of the glasslike wand down on the waist-high metal slab on which I had been laying. It would not break. I lashed out at the advancing creatures, screaming desperate threats at them.

I shouted wildly, "Get away from me! What are you?"

The creatures slowed but continued toward me with their hands outstretched. [See the artist's picture.]

"Keep back, damn you!" I shrieked. They halted. In a snarling crouch I held the tube threateningly back behind my head. I felt hopelessly trapped. I was surrounded, with my back to the wall.

There was a door behind the nightmarish beings. To get out I was going to have to go through them.

It was a standoff. I crouched slightly on my trembling legs, the cold sweat pouring off me. My mind was a whirling confusion of terror.

The creatures stood silently staring at me. I could hardly bear to look at them, but I got my first good look at them.

They just stood there mutely. They were a little under five feet in height. They had the basic humanoid form, consisting of two legs, two arms, and hands with five fingers on each. They had a head with the normal human arrangement of features. But other than that, their similarity to humans quickly became terrifyingly obscure.

Their thin bones were covered with white marshmallowy-looking flesh. They had on single-piece coverall type suits that seemed to be made of soft suede-like material of an orangish-brown color. I could not see any grain in the material like cloth would have. In fact, their clothes did not even appear to have any seams. I saw no buttons, zippers, or snaps. They wore no belts around their middles. The loose billowy garments were gathered at the wrists and perhaps the ankles. They didn't have any kind of raised collar at the neck either.

They wore simple pinkish-tan footwear. I could not make out the details of what their shoes were like, but they had very small feet, about size four by my measure.

When they extended their hands toward me, I noticed they had no nails on their fingers. Their hands were small, delicate, and without hair. Their thin round fingers were unwrinkled.

The thin membrane of their skin was stretched over the curves of their small bodies without wrinkles. The bends of their fingers and necks made very small, slightly rounded folds instead of sharp creases.

Their bald heads were disproportionately large for the size of their bodies. They had bulging, oversized craniums, a small jaw structure, and an underdeveloped appearance to their features that was almost infantile. Their thin-lipped mouths were narrow and I never saw them open.

Close to their heads on either side were the tiny crinkled lobes of their ears. Their miniature rounded noses had small oval nostrils.

The only feature that was not underdeveloped were those incredible eyes! Those glistening brown orbs had irises twice the size of a normal human eye. The iris, or colored part of the eye, was nearly an inch in diameter! The iris was so large that even parts of the pupils were hidden by the lids, giving the eyes a certain cat-like appearance. There was very little of the white part of the eye showing. They had no lashes and no eyebrows.

The occasional blink in their eyes was striking. Their huge lids slid quickly down over the glassy bubbles of their eyes, then flipped over again like the release of roll-up window shades. These moist, lashless eyes and the milky translucence of their skin made their appearance slightly reminiscent of a cave salamander. But strangely, in spite of my terror, I felt there was something gentle and familiar about them. In fact, their overall look was disturbingly like that of a human fetus.

Their sharp gaze alternately darted about and then fixed me with an intense stare, a look so piercing that it seemed they were seeing right through me. I felt naked and exposed under their scrutiny.

The proceeding description of the aliens is the most comprehensive that the author has ever seen, and this happened in 1975, well before abduction became a common happening.

I could not stand to look at their eyes, but I found my own kept returning to look into theirs. It was impossible to avoid their compelling stare. Those eyes were the creepiest, most frightening things I had seen in my entire life.

I've got to get out of here! My mind seized on that one driving, panicked thought. I had to get away from those awful monsters, away from those horrid eyes! I felt desperate to escape. Desperate to return to the open forest that I thought must be somewhere just outside this stifling place.

With all the screaming and hysterical questions I had thrown at them, they never once said anything to me. I did not hear them speak to each other. Their mouths never made any kind of sound. The only sounds I heard were those of movements and my own voice.

Those three silent beings were between me and the only apparent way out. I gathered every ounce of energy I had to fight for my life.

What am I going to do? I thought wildly. *If I can, I'll just push them out of the way and run past them...but the thought of touching them is so revolting!* I thought. I didn't have the slightest idea of what they were capable of doing to me. They could have hidden weapons or even venom or something weird like that.

I only knew I had to get away from them and get out of there, even though the prospect of battling my way past them was utterly terrifying.

Just as I girded myself to spring at them, they abruptly turned and scurried out of the room! They went out of the open door, turned right, and disappeared.

It is apparent from the hundreds and probably thousands of abductions that have taken place that the type of aliens that Travis is encountering has the ability to perform telepathy and mind reading. Thus, they anticipated his future movement and decided to leave the immediate area.

The anticlimax of their retreat was incredible. The extra adrenaline that had squirted into my blood stream now had me trembling uncontrollably. I collapsed back against the bench and struggled to slow my racing heart. I gulped the heavy air in ragged gasps.

Slowly, I began to recover. Breathing deeply, I looked around me. I was in an irregular room with metal walls. The floor and ceiling were shaped like a piece of pie with the point bitten off. The ceiling was about seven feet high. Three of the walls were all about twelve feet in length. Two of these were straight with a concave one between them. The two straight walls were not parallel but intersected another smaller curved wall on the other end. The smaller curved wall was convex and was about eight feet wide. It had an open doorway in it that was about three feet by six and half feet.

The metal of the walls had a textured, matte-gray appearance. The surface was dull and nonreflective. I saw no bolts, rivets, screws, or seams of any kind. The surface of the walls, floors, and ceiling just curved into each other. Even the light fixtures, the curving bench, and the table simply curved into the surface to which they were attached. In fact, everything seemed to be molded out of a single, continuous piece of material!

In his book, *Behind the Flying Saucers*, author Frank Scully was told by Dr. Gee (an assumed name) of three flying saucers that had come down. At least two of the three downed ships were too large to be moved, and the Air Force, in wanting to move the ships, decided to dismantle them because they were too big to move otherwise.

This became a most interesting study. There was nothing on the outer skin that would indicate how the ship was put together.

After a long study it was found that the ship was assembled in segments. The segments fit into grooves and were pinned together at the base.

In general, the room was drab and featureless. It was devoid of ornamentation or color. There were no windows or ventilation openings. I noticed no cupboards, closets, or other doors. I couldn't see any buttons, switches, or electrical receptacles on the walls. The small room contained only the light fixture, the table, the narrow counter I leaned on, and the device that had fallen off my chest.

The device had quit rocking back and forth by now and just lay there next to the table. The odd glow still came from under the edges of it. When it had fallen, it had hit the floor with a loud noise. Curiously, the floor did not clang or ring. For a metal room, the acoustics seemed quite normal—that is, flat and non-echoing. The floor and table only thudded deeply when I stepped on or struck the surfaces. The metal seemed to be very thick and dense.

The table I had been laying on was a slab of metal too, about an inch and a half thick and approximately six and a half feet in length. It had a single round leg about four inches in diameter that curved into the floor like it had grown there.

The light was similarly suspended by a single descending, two-inch column that curved into the surfaces of the ceiling.

Thinking that I heard a sound, I whirled, jerking my head around and riveting my eyes on the door. I halted in the opening.

I took a deep breath. I felt a little stronger, but the pain still hammered relentlessly in my head and especially my chest. I was sweating and the heavy air was difficult to breathe.

"I have got to get out of here!" I thought frantically.

There was a curving hallway about three feet wide passing by the door outside. The ceiling of the hall gave off a faint, almost unnoticeable illumination. I looked to the right down the narrow dimly lit passage in the direction the aliens had vanished. There was no one in sight.

Seeing nothing in the passage to my left, I began walking that way. I broke into a frightened run down the narrow corridor.

The cramped hallway turned continuously in a tight curve to the right. I dashed past an open doorway on my left, without looking in. It was only ten feet down the hall from the door I had just left. I caught the glimpse of a room but was afraid to stop.

Wait just a damned minute, Travis! I said to myself. *What if I missed a chance at that doorway to find a way out of this place?* I saw another doorway ten more feet ahead on my right. I slowed down to a walk as I neared it. I stopped in the opening.

I looked in cautiously. I saw a round room about sixteen feet across with a domed ceiling about ten feet high. There was no one in there. The room was totally empty except for a single chair that faced away from me. I looked behind me. The hallway was still empty in both directions. I slowly entered the room. I hesitated to approach the high-backed chair directly. There could be somebody sitting in it that I could not see!

I circled, keeping my distance from the chair but checking to see if anyone was sitting there. I followed the curve of the wall to get around to where I could see the side of the chair. With much relief I saw that the chair was unoccupied.

Glancing apprehensively toward the open door, I slowly went toward the chair. As I gradually approached it, a very curious thing began to happen.

The closer I got to it, the darker the room became! Small points of light became visible on or through the walls or even the floor. I stepped back and the effect diminished. I stepped forward and it increased again. The points of light became brighter in contrast to the darkening background. It was like the stars coming into view in the evening, only much faster. The matte-gray of the metal wall faded out to be replaced by the glinting, speckled deep-black of space.

I thought, *Maybe this is a planetarium type of project or....good grief! What if this is actually some kind of viewing screen showing where this thing is at!*

I was suddenly gripped with the fear that even if I did find a way outside, I would die in the airlessness of space.

I looked at the controls on the chair. Maybe, just maybe, one of the buttons would open a door or something. I moved closer and studied the array of switches. On the left arm there was a single, short, thick lever with a T grip. Trembling, I sat on the hard, slightly curved surface of the chair. This put the short lever on my left. I put my hand on its molded T grip. The brown handle was slightly small for my hand. The whole chair was a little too small.

From where I sat, I could see stars all around me, even on the wall where I had just come through the door. The surfaces of the room were only faintly visible, but the doorway I had come through was as clear as ever. I could see clouds of tiny stars and dust in a band like the Milky Way. Only it was more distinct than I had seen it on a clear night in the woods.

Well, here goes," I said to myself. I rotated the handle of the lever forward. I felt suddenly disoriented as the star began moving downward in front of me, in unison. Pulled my hand quickly out of the lever and the stars stopped moving. The handle slowly returned to its original position. The stars did not return to their original positions, however, but remained where they were.

"Damn! Something has to work!" I said, still trying to find a way out of this thing.

I got out of the chair and walked to the edge of the room. As I did the stars faded out and the surfaces of the wall, ceiling, and floor came in to better view. I searched the edges of the room for a switch or an opening mechanism. I saw none. Then I heard a faint sound.

I whirled around and looked at the door. There standing in the doorway was a human being!

I stood frozen on the spot. He was a man about six feet, two inches tall. His helmeted head barely missed the top of the doorway. He was extremely muscular and evenly proportioned. He looked to weigh about two hundred pounds. He wore a tight-fitting bright blue suit of material that looked like soft velour. His feet were covered with black boots and a black band or belt was wrapped around his middle. He carried no tools or weapons on his belt or in his hand. There was no insignia on his clothing.

Wow! How did he get here? Is he from the Air Force? What's going on here? Maybe he is from NASA! I'm saved. Another human—one of my own kind! Relief flooded over me. I was never before so glad to see a total stranger.

The man gestured with his right hand for me to come toward him. He beckoned with his open hand.

I ran up to him, exclaiming and babbling all sorts of questions.

"How did you get here? Can you get me out of here? There were these terrible things in here. What's going on? Who are you? Please help me!"

The man remained silent throughout my verbal barrage. I was worried by his silence. I looked at his face closely through the helmet.

He had coarse, sandy-blond hair of medium length that covered his ears. He had a dark complexion, like a deep, even tan. He had no beard or mustache. In fact, I couldn't even see stubble or dark shadows of whiskers. He had slightly rugged, masculine features and strange eyes. They were a bright, golden-hazel color, but there was still something else that I could not quite place.

The aforementioned description of the man with the sandy-blond hair that covered his ears, with a dark complexion like a deep tan, and no facial hair will be repeated for three other individuals later in this Travis Walton story. Two will be male and one will be female. They all looked alike in a familial sort of way, although they were not identical. The female wore her hair longer. But, more importantly, later on in an abduction story by Budd Hopkins, there will be a description of a boy with light brown-blond hair with blue eyes, as well as in another UFO experience by Edward "Billy" Mieir in which he met with a female space person numerous times with blond hair and blue eyes.

His helmet was like a transparent sphere that was slightly flattened. It had no tubes or hoses connected to it. It had a wide black rim that rested down closely over the contour of his shoulders.

The man did not offer any acknowledgement to my questions. He only smiled kindly in a tolerant manner. He did not appear to have any intention of answering me.

Then it hit me. *That's it! Of course he can't answer with that helmet on. He probably can't even hear me!*

He took me firmly, but gently, by the left arm and gestured for me to go with him. He seemed friendly enough. He probably just wanted to get someplace where he could remove his helmet. Anyway, he was too big to argue with. It was good to be in the company of a real human being. I knew one thing for sure: if I could get out of there and away from where those aliens lurked, I was going to be cooperative.

He took me out of that room and hurried me down the narrow hallway, pulling me along behind him because of its narrowness. He stopped in front of a closed door that slid open to his right in the wall. I did not see what caused it to open.

The door opened to a bare room that was so small that it was more like a foyer or a section of a hallway. The door slid shut quickly and silently behind us.

We spent approximately two minutes in the metal cubical, which was only about seven by five by twelve feet. Then an opposite door slid open to the right. Brilliant warm light and fresh, cool air wafted in that reminded me of springtime in the out-of-doors.

The side walls of the passage outside the door sloped down at the forty-five degree angle to meet a ramp that continued to slope downward.

I looked around to discover that, although I was outside that dim, humid craft, I was not outdoors. I was in a huge room. The ceiling itself curved down to form one of the larger walls in the room. The room was shaped like one quarter of a cylinder laid on its side.

The outside of the craft we had just left was shaped like the one we had seen in the woods. It was about sixty feet in diameter and sixteen feet high, much larger than the one that had zapped me in the woods.

On my left, toward one end of the large room, there were two or three oval-shaped saucers that were reflective like highly polished chrome. They looked to be about forty to forty-five feet in diameter.

As I mentioned at the end of *Behind the Flying Saucers*, many large cylindrical or cigar-shaped mother ships have been seen that have the ability to store and discharge smaller saucer-shaped ships. That is, without a doubt, what Travis has now entered.

The man escorted Travis across the open floor toward double sliding doors. The doors opened quickly from the middle outward. We were in a wide hallway about six feet wide. The hallway was straight and perhaps eight feet long. There were double doors distributed along the hallway but the doors were closed.

"When do I get to go home?" I asked. "Where are we going now?"

No reply.

At the end of the hallway, there was another set of double doors. The doors slid silently back from the middle.

We entered a white room approximately fifteen feet square with an eight-foot ceiling. The room had a table and a chair in it, but the first thing I noticed were three other humans!

Two men and a woman were standing around the table. They were all wearing velvety blue uniforms like the one the first man had worn, except they had no helmets.

The two men had the same muscularity and the same masculine good looks as the first man. The woman also had a face and figure that was typical of her sex. They were smooth-skinned and had no blemishes. No moles, freckles, wrinkles, or scars marked their skin. They looked alike in a familial sort of way, although they were not identical.

They all had the same coarse, brownish-blond hair. The woman wore hers longer than the men, past her shoulders. She did not appear to wear make-up. They seemed to be in their mid-twenties, perhaps older. They all had those golden-hazel eyes. There was definitely something odd about the eyes; I just could not tell what it was.

I started talking to them, trying to get them to answer.

"Would somebody please tell me where I am?" I asked. I was still shaken from my encounter with those awful creatures. "What in hell is going on? What is this place?"

They did not answer me. They only looked at me, although not unkindly. The helmeted man sat me down in the chair. He then crossed the room to a door and when it opened, he went out. There was a corridor outside the door; there he turned right.

The table was a shiny blackslab with a single silvery leg about six inches in diameter. It was about seven feet by three and a half feet across and two inches thick, and had rounded edges and corners.

A man and the woman came around the table and approached me. They stood on either side of the chair I was sitting in.

"What are you doing?" I asked.

Silently they each took me by an arm and led me toward the table. I did not know why I should cooperate with them, but I was in no position to argue, so I went along at first.

They lifted me easily onto the edge of the table. I became wary and started protesting.

"Wait a minute..." I started. "Just tell me what you are going to do!"

I began to resist them. But all three began pushing me back down on the table. I looked up at the ceiling, which was totally covered with panels of softly glowing white light with a faint blue cast.

From out of nowhere I saw that the woman suddenly had an object in her hand that looked like one of those clear, soft-plastic oxygen masks. Only there were no tubes connected to it.

She pressed the mask down over my mouth and nose. I started to reach up to pull it away.

Before I could complete the motion, I got weak and everything started getting gray. Then there was nothing at all, but oblivious blackness.

The End of Chapter 3

Consciousness returned to me on the night of November 10, 1975. I woke to find myself on the cold pavement west of Heber, Arizona.

Roswell—Area S4—and Alien Technology

Withheld for Six Decades

Roswell
The proof I will present of a crash of an alien craft
at Roswell consists of two testimonials

Testimonial No. 1
Jesse Marcel, Sr.

In 1947 he was one of two people who went to Mac Bracel's ranch and picked up a load of debris from the alien craft. Later he was forced by Brigadier General Rodger Ramey to identify pieces of a weather balloon as what he had picked up at the ranch. He had been trying to set the record straight ever since.

In 1980 he got his chance, when actually at the debris field (now totally cleaned up) a video recording was made of him, which was shown on a television program called "Showtime" on July 31, 1994. I recorded that show and have a permanent record of it. This is what he said.

"What I saw I couldn't believe, there was so much of it. So we proceeded to pick up as much of it as we could, the debris, and loaded it in the wagon.

"It was not anything from this Earth, because I was the intelligence officer and I was familiar with all the materials in aircraft and in our air travels."

Jesse Marcel died in 1986.

Quoted from a UFO Central video
by Donald R. Schmitt

Testimonial No. 2
Mr. Frank Kaufman was assigned to a special military
intelligence unit at the Roswell Air Base in 1947

This is Don Schmitt's interview with Mr. Frank Kaufman.

"Well, Don, let me explain that at that time the Army Air Force base at Roswell was one of the most important bases because of many varied activities going on there. We had the Norton bomb sight there; it was the training base of the 509th Bomb Group that had dropped the atomic bomb on Japan. You had experimental work going on at White Sands and also highly secret work going on at Los Alamos in the northern part of the state. So you can see this was a hotbed of activity; it was one of the hottest places in the entire world. Well, in June of 1947 our radar people that were from White Sands noticed a series of erratic movements of blips on the night of July the 4th. We were watching the blips; it must have been about 11:00 P.M. There was a severe thunderstorm and heavy rain going on in the entire area. The screen lit up; the radar man just could not make out what was wrong. Maybe there was something wrong with the radar screen, but he was told it was in working order. So he came to the conclusion that something went down east of White Sands, where he did not know. So in the meantime, we were in constant communication. What caught our attention was that something went down north of Roswell and that people driving on US 285 North going south noticed an orange ball falling toward Earth. Well, it was common in those days to call the base and tell them that something unusual was happening. In the meantime we got back to the base and Major Easley, the Provost Marshall, sent some MPs out on 285 to locate where this orange ball actually fell to Earth. And they noticed this orange glow off the highway, maybe 15 miles off the highway, and when we arrived back to the base we were told to go out there to the area. We had searchlights and what have you. We had to clip wire fences to get into the area and what we saw at that time was just unbelievable. It wasn't one of our craft—we know what they look like—but what we saw was a craft of unknown origin!"

Eyewitness Frank Kaufman talked more about
the Roswell cover up with Don Schmitt.

"Well, after we got most of the craft and the bodies cleared out of the impact area and onto the base hospital and hanger 84, we convened into Colonel

Blanchared's conference room to determine how we were going to handle the press, you know. And there was quite a few out there that were wanting some answers, and, well, how do you explain something like that? It's something unheard of, and we didn't know anything about a UFO or a flying disc or anything that was extraterrestrial or what have you. So after a couple of hours we finally came to the conclusion—in fact, it was Major Thomas that came up with the idea—that maybe if we tell them the truth and take a chance on whether they would believe it or not. So we agreed to that, and it was rather interesting. When we went out of the conference room and met members of the media there—there must have been about 25 or 30—and Thomas started off very nicely. He said, 'Ladies and gentlemen, the announcement that I have is that we have been invaded from outer space. We have a craft, possibly of extraterrestrial origin.' When he said that, about two-thirds of the group just busted out laughing and threw up their hands and said, 'Oh, the hell with this.' And they thought we were going to come up with some cockamamy story and they just left the room. But the small group that stayed there weren't satisfied; they wanted to know something about the extraterrestrials. Thomas said, 'I don't know anything. I'm just telling you, we haven't actually made a thorough examination of the craft or the bodies or anything of that nature. And until such a time, we will have to leave it as it is.' Well, when we went back to the conference room—Blanchard and Major Easley, the Provost Marshall, and Jesse Marcel the intelligence officer, and the rest of us—and we said, 'By God, the plan worked.' The truth, you know, and thats the way we did it, because we had no idea what the paper was going to say. The paper said that a flying disc was captured and, of course, the next day Ramey came out contradicting the flying disc story and said it was a weather balloon. Well, we know what a weather balloon looks like, and we know what our plane looked like, but a craft of unknown origin is something else."

Don Schmitt commented, "Tell us about the bodies and the craft itself."

"There were five bodies—one was outside; one was partially outside; the other three were inside the craft. The craft itself was maybe 20 or 25 feet in length and maybe 6 feet in height and 15 feet in width. There was a metallic smell around the craft. Inside the craft was a bluish, greenish light. There was a console in front and a little console in the back of the craft. I didn't go through the craft with a fine-tooth comb. I didn't spend that much time checking out all

details because we had to get that damn thing out of there before daylight. Well, we got it on a flatbed and we had a hell of a time getting out of the area because of the mud and we were sliding all over the place. We put a tarp over it and part of the craft was exposed, and we went right down main street. They would think it was another plane and stuff like that. We didn't hide anything. And we went in the back entrance of the base, back to hanger 84, and that is where it was unloaded lickety-split. No fanfare, no band, no flag waving, or anything of that nature."

**"Tell me about the aliens, were they
good-looking people?" Don inquired.**

"Oh yeah, they didn't have any slanted eyes or horny fingers. I don't know whether you want to call them people—I call them people. They were good-looking people, fine skin, kind of ash colored. Eyes were a little bit larger than ours, more pronounced. Small nose, small mouth, very small ears, no hair, very fine features. Very well built, maybe five-four or five-five in height."

**"In your personal opinion, what happened here in 1947
in Roswell? What is your bottom line?" asked Don.**

"That in 1947—I can only put it this way—that a craft of unknown origin crashed north of Roswell. It was recovered with bodies not of this Earth, which proved that we are not alone in this vast universe of ours."

**The following is a list of six government projects that may
prove that the two testimonial statements are lies.**

1 Weather balloon
2 Project Mogul, enormous balloons
3 Operation Hydive—dummies
4 Project Excellsor—high altitude jumps by humans
5 Monkey space biology
6 Ventricular vehicles

Which would you pick, the two testimonials or one of the above six?

Area S4 and alien technology,
withheld for six decades

John Lear, holder of 17 flight records and having 16,000 hours of flying time, tells of his involvement with Bob Lazar. His account follows.

In the summer of 1988 I was having a house appraised and the appraiser, who was interested in UFOs and particularly the rumors of alien UFOs in Area S4 on the Nellis Air Force Range, wanted the opinion of this scientist of what he thought about the rumors. At that time I was doing a lot of lecturing and there was lot of publicity about me and UFOs, so I met this gentleman, Bob Lazar, and he didn't believe the rumors at all. He told me that he worked at Los Alamos and had a Q clearance and a number of other compartmental clearances. He knew a lot of secret things and he said that if there had been a cover-up about UFOs in Area S4 he would have known about it. So over the next three or four months we got to know Bob very well and he got to know us. We passed him various information, which he checked out with the people he knew who still worked at Los Alamos, specifically people who had access to the classified library. Bob told that Project Grudge, which the Air Force told the public was cancelled in 1949, was still active. He was able to determine through his friend, who had access to the classified library, that it was still going on. I had mentioned that one of the aliens we had captured was kept at a secret place called yy-2 facility, and he had found out that there was a classified mail stop at Los Alamos called yy-2. Now that does not mean that it was kept daily up there, but it shows that I knew secret things that were going on. There was enough evidence there that he thought, well, maybe there is something to this and he wanted to find out. So being the highly educated person that he was—he held two master's degrees at MIT and also knew Dr. Keller, who was the father of the H bomb. He was able to send his resume to Dr. Keller, who called him and asked him where he wanted to work. Dr. Keller said he knew of two places—either EG&G Las Vegas or Lawrence Livermore Laboratories in California. Bob said, "I want to work in Area 51."

The reason he wanted to go there was to get as close as he could to where we thought the saucer testing was going on. Well, during the next six weeks after that he was contacted by EG&G. He was given three security interviews and three interviews on his basic knowledge, and they were so impressed with his performance that they went ahead and hired him.

On December 6, 1988, Bob came here in the evening as he usually did. I was sitting here writing checks, and he sat right in that seat. I said, "What's going on Bob,"

He said, "I saw a disc today."

I was so startled I thought I didn't hear him and I said, "What?"

He said, "I saw a disc today."

I said, "Theirs or ours?"

And he said, "Theirs."

I said, "You went to the test site?"

He said, "Yeah, I just got back; it's the first time I went up there."

I said, "Oh, my God, what are you doing here? Don't jeopardize your security clearance. Work up there for a while and find out what's going on."

He said, "No, you have taken so much flak over this thing I am going to tell you exactly what I saw."

For the next 3 hours and 47 minutes he proceeded to tell me exactly what he saw on his first trip to S4. Basically it was that we had nine extra-terrestrial vehicles. He told me about the power plants; he told me he had been briefed on the aliens that flew them; he told me he had been briefed on a number of other secret things; he told me that we did have a secret base on the moon; he told me that we also had a base on Mars.

As far as the supposed base on the moon goes, there was a probe sent to the moon in, I believe, 1998 called Clementine. You would assume that such a probe would be sent by NASA, but instead it was sent by the U.S. Air Force. This probe took several thousand pictures of the moon, but the only picture that was for public viewing was the one showing the edge of the moon, where it has constant sunshine, because this would be an ideal place to have a settlement. The other thousands of pictures were never shown. This, of course, does not prove that they have a base on the moon, but they certainly must be hiding something.

The next part is taken from a video titled "The Lazar Tape"

It starts out by having a sports car pull up to the forefront on a gravel road in the countryside. The door opens and a man gets out and says the following:

Hi. I am Bob Lazar. During 1988 and early 1989 I worked on the propulsion systems of extraterrestrial vehicles for the United States government. The hardware and technology I was exposed to should be placed in the proper hands of the scientific community. It is the right of every person on Earth to know that there is physical evidence that proves that there is life elsewhere and at least one form of that life has been here.

For those of you who are limited to information about me, I'll give you a brief background. I am a physicist; I have degrees in physics and electronic technology. I worked in a number of scientific programs, some of which required top secret and above top secret security clearances. The part that is easily verifiable is that of my early-1980s job at the Los Alamos Meson Physics Facility in Los Alamos, New Mexico. Between December of '88 and April of '89 I worked as a senior staff physicist at what is the most secret project in history. My place of work was a facility known in the area as S4 on the Nellis Air Force Range in central Nevada. Area S4 is located approximately 15 miles south of the infamous Area 51 installation at Groom Lake, where the U2 and the SR71 spy planes were developed. For the duration of my employment at S4 I was paid by the United States Navy.

In this video I will deal with information with which I have hands-on experience and personal instruction. In other words, not only did I read briefing reports and not only was I taught the theories of these technologies, but they were demonstrated for me and I know that they were true and accurate. Some of the points covered in this section will be:

1. How vast distances of space are traveled by virtue of an intense gravitational field
2. How this gravitational field is generated
3. What the power source is and how it functions
4. General information about discs and project at S4.

This information is being conveyed to you as it was to me with the exception that in most cases I have simplified things for those of you with non-technological backgrounds. So let's begin.

At the beginning of this first session I am going to give you three short science lessons. Once you have learned them you will not only know more about interstellar travel than most anyone else in the world, you will know the actual method another civilization has used to travel from another star system to the planet Earth.

Now, during the course of this, I am going to tell you about information that I have learned at S4, the information that we are already aware of, and when I say "we" I mean the general mainstream scientific community. One of the most frequently asked questions is: How is it possible to cross vast expenses of space without exceeding the speed of light? Or how can you travel with a reasonable time and economy between points that are light years apart? Now keep in mind that the speed of light is 186,000 miles per second, which translates into roughly to 669,000,000 miles per hour, and a light year is the distance traveled in one year at the speed of light. Centuri, which is the star system nearest ours, would take four years at the speed of light. So up until now when we have examined the requirements to travel these distances we have always had to consider the problem of having to travel at the speed of light. This poses a problem with propulsion, navigation, fuel capacities. And even when you consider the effects of acceleration on space-time—which includes time dilation, mass increase, and lane contraction, and whole list of other things—it quickly becomes evident that this type of travel is impractical!

The truth of the matter is that traveling these distances requires a level of technology that man has not achieved, but it has nothing to do with traveling in a linear mode near the speed of light. We know that the shortest distance between two points is a straight line. So in our universe we have always assumed that the fastest way to travel from point A to point B is to travel in a straight line at the speed of light. Well, the fact is, when you are dealing with space-time and you enjoy the capability of generating an intense gravitational field, the fastest way from point A to point B is to distort or warp or bend the space-time between point A and point B, thereby bringing point A and point B closer together. The more intense the gravitational field, the greater the distortion of space-time and shorter the distance between point A and point B.

In France in 1859, Urbain Gean Le Verrier, director of the Paris Observatory and imperial mathematician, using Newton's Laws of Gravity, unveiled a problem with the motion of the planet Mercury. The indications were of a planet closer to the Sun than Mercury. Incredibly, the prediction was immediately fulfilled by an obscure country doctor named Edmond Modeste Lescarbault, using a homemade telescope. The newly discovered planet was named Vulcan for the Roman God of Fire. However, it was no sooner discovered than it was lost. Still, it reappeared often enough to tantalize even the skeptics into considering its existence.

Through the years several famous astronomers tried to calculate an answer to the problem.

In 1846, Ubain Gean Le Verrier was made famous by the discovery of the planet Neptune by using Newton's law of gravity and the residuals of the planet Uranus. However, as it all turned out, Newton's law did not apply to Mercury.

In 1915 Albert Einstein had just introduced new gravitational equations derived from his General Theory of Relativity. Simply put, he proposed that in the neighborhood of small bodies such as the Earth, the relativistic adjustments to Newton's law is negligble, but close to a massive body such as the Sun, there is a significant curvature of Einsteinian space-time, which produces a non-Newtonian warp in the trajectory of nearby bodies such as Mercury. Einstein found that according to his theory of gravitation, Mercury should process slightly faster than the Newtonian rate. In fact, the excess comes out to 0.1 arc seconds for each orbital revolution of the planet, or 43 arc seconds per century; this calculated value was identical to the 43 arc seconds found by Simond Newcomb.

After making this calculation, Einstein later confessed, he was for several days beside himself with excitement.

Einstein's calculations of the advance of the perihelion of Mercury was one of the most dramatic early triumphs of General Relativity. The case of Mercury is perhaps the most satisfying proof of the correctness of Einstein's ideas.

This is an explanation of space-time travel taken out of the contact notes of Edward Billy Meier.

The hyper-drive, as you call it, is a drive which generates a million-fold, a billion-fold the speed of light, thus the hyper-speed by which hyper-space is penetrated. A space in which the mass increases in relation to speed. So time and space collapses and they become zero time and zero space. This means time and space cease to exist. And exactly by that distances of numerous light-years are traversed in a fraction of a second, with no time lag.

Well indeed space-time is an entity, and one of its properties is that it can be distorted or bent by a gravitational field. We know that gravity bends or distorts space-time by virtue of the fact that we are able to see stars that we know should be blocked from our view by the Sun. This is made possible because the Sun's gravitational field distorts the space-time and light around the Sun, allowing us to view stars that should be hidden from view. We know that gravity distorts time by virtue of the fact that if we take two identical atomic clocks and keep one at sea level and take the other to a high altitude—when we bring them both back together they reflect different times. The difference in the passage of time is explained by the fact that a gravitational field weakens the further you get from the sources, so the atomic clock that was taken to the high altitude to less powerful gravitational field than the clock which we kept at sea level. The effect of a gravitational field on space-time is something that we have been able to observe but not able to experiment with. This is due to our inability to generate a gravitational field. Up until this point in time, a great mass such as a star, planet, or moon was the only source of a large gravitational field that we were aware of. So just as a gravitational field around a great mass distorts space-time, any gravitational field, weather naturally occurring or generated, distorts space-time in a similar manner.

Now, the great benefit of generating an intense gravitational field is not only can you turn it on, but you can turn it off.

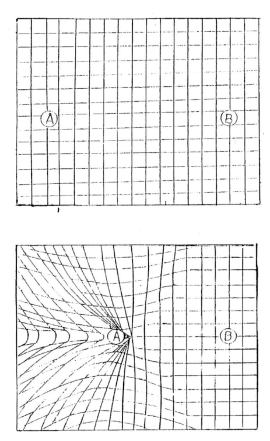

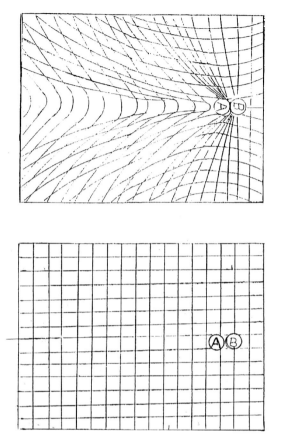

Now, referring to the space-time illustrations, we can see that when we generate an intense gravitational field we can distort space-time and, in turn, the distance between the point where we are and the point where we want to be. We can then position ourselves to the point where we want to be and then stop generating the gravitational field allowing space-time to return to its natural form. In this manner we can travel great distances with little linear movement, and this is how space-time distortion translates into reduced distance.

The next question is how do you generate a gravitational field. Up until this point in time I have used the term *generate* to describe the capability of producing a gravitational field. But since I am not aware of any way of creating a gravitational field from nothing, a more accurate term may be *to access and amplify a gravitational field*, and this is what I mean when I use the term *generate*. To understand how gravity is generated or accessed and amplified you must first know what gravity is. There are two main theories—the wave theory, which states that gravity is a wave, and the currently accepted theory of gravitons, which are alleged subatomic particles that perform as gravity, which just isn't so. Well, gravity is a wave, and there are two specific different types of gravity—gravity A and gravity B. Gravity A works on a smaller micro scale, while gravity B works on a larger macro scale. We are familiar with gravity B; it is the big gravity wave that holds Earth as well as the rest of the planets in orbit around the Sun and holds the moon as well as man-made satellites in orbit around the Earth. We are not familiar with gravity A; it is the small gravity wave which is the major contributing force that holds together the mass that makes up all protons and neutrons. Gravity A is currently being labeled as the strong nucleus force in mainstream physics, and gravity A is the wave that you need to access and amplify to enable you to cause space-time distortion for inter-stellar travel.

To keep them straight, just remember that gravity A works on an atomic scale and gravity B is the big gravity wave that works on a stellar or planetary level. However, don't mistake the size of the waves for their strength, because gravity A is a much stronger force than gravity B. You can momentarily break the gravity B field by simply jumping in the air, so this is not an intense gravitational field. Locating gravity A is no problem because it is found in the nucleus of every atom of all matter here on Earth and all matter anywhere else in our universe. However, accessing gravity A with the naturally occurring atoms here on Earth is a big problem. Actually, I am not aware of any way of accessing the gravity A wave using any of the Earth's elements, whether naturally occurring or synthesized, and here's why.

We have already learned that gravity A is a major force that holds together the mass that makes up protons and neutrons. This means the gravity A wave we are trying to access is virtually inexcessible, as it is located within matter or at least within the matter we have here on Earth.

However, the Earth is not representative of all matter that is within our universe. The residual matter that remains after the creation of a solar system is totally dependent on contributing factors which were present during the creation of a solar system. The two main factors which determine what residual matter remains after the creation of a solar system are the amount of electromagnetic energy and the amount of mass present during the solar systems creation. Our solar system has one star which is our Sun, but the majority of solar systems in our Milky Way galaxy are binary and multiple star systems. In fact, many single star systems have suns that are so large that our sun would appear to be a dwarf in comparison. Keeping all this in mind, it should be obvious that a large single star system, binary star system, or multiple star system would have all of the prerequisite mass present during their creation—this makes it possible for these systems to possess elements that are not native to Earth.

Scientists have long theorized that there are potential combinations of protons and neutrons which should provide stable elements with atomic numbers higher than any which appear on the periodic chart, although none of the heavy elements appear naturally here on Earth. Eighty-eight of the first 92 elements on the periodic chart appear naturally here on Earth. Some elements do appear in trace amounts, but for the most part we synthesize the heavier elements in laboratories. Generally speaking, the stability of these synthesized heavy elements decrease as their atomic numbers increase, but experiments for heavy ion research in Germany have shown that this may only be true up to certain point because the half life of element 109 is longer than that of element 108. The point is that our observation and theories are accurate.

The fact is that heavier stable elements with higher atomic numbers which have more protons, neutrons, and electrons do exist. However, up until this point in history, there has been no physical evidence to prove this. But now the proof is here. The most important attribute of these heavier stable elements is that the gravity A wave is so abundant that it actually extends past the perimeter of the atom. These heavier stable elements literally have their own gravity A field around them in addition to the gravity B field that is native to all elements. No naturally occurring atoms on Earth have enough protons and neutrons for the accumulative A wave to extend past the perimeter of the atom so you can access it. Even though the distance the gravity A wave extends is infinitesimal, it is accessible and it has amplitude, wave length, and frequency, just like any other wave in the electromagnetic spectrum. Once you can access the gravity A wave you can amplify it just like any other electromagnetic wave.

What is the power source for space travel?

How is it possible to have a compact, lightweight, onboard power source that can provide the vast amount of power required for space-time distortion?

For everyone to understand this I need to further explain a couple of things we briefly touched upon. I said for the most part we synthesize or create heavier elements in excellerators and their stability decreases as their atomic numbers increase.

So what does all this mean? Well, we synthesize these heavier unstable elements by using more stable elements as targets in a particle excellerator. We then bombard the target with various atomic and sub-atomic particles; at this point transmutation takes place, making the target element a different heavier element. This element now has a different higher atomic number, as the atomic number indicates the number of protons in the nucleus of the atom. So this is what I mean when I say their atomic number increases. What does their stability decreases mean? The length of time which an element exists before it decays determines its stability. Atoms of some elements decay faster than atoms of other elements, so the faster an element decays it releases or radiates sub-atomic particles and energy, which is the radiation that a Geiger counter detects.

Those elements in which nuclear radiation can be detected are radioactive elements. These heavy elements, which are synthesized in particle excellerators, are radioactive, and they decay very rapidly. Hence, we are only able to make a few atoms of these elements, and because they decay so rapidly we are not able to observe much about them. This is what I mean when I say their stability decreases. However, there are elements with higher atomic numbers which are stable even though they don't occur naturally on Earth, and we can't synthesize them in particle excellerators.

These are the elements in the 114 and 115 range, which don't appear on the periodic chart. Beyond the element 115 the elements become unstable again, and in fact element 116 decays in a fraction of a second. This finally brings us to the power source. The power source is a reactor which uses the element 115 as its fuel. In the reactor element 115 is used as the target and is bombarded with protons in a small particle excellerator. When a proton plugs into the nucleus of an atom of 115 it increases its atomic number and becomes an element of 116, which, remember, decays instantly. What an element of 116 radiates is anti-matter.

What is anti-matter? Anti-matter is the exact counterpart of matter, which has a charge that is the opposite of matter. When combined with matter in our universe, anti-matter completely converts to energy and that is what we generally call an explosion.

So back to our power source.

So back to our power source

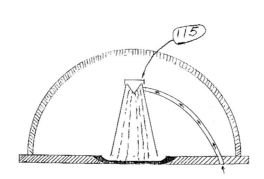

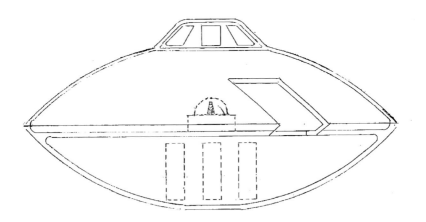

Inside the reactor the element of 115 is bombarded with a proton, which plugs in the nucleus of the 115 atom and becomes the element 116, which immediately decays or radiates or releases small amounts of anti-matter. The anti-matter is released into a vacuum in a tuned tube, which keeps it from reacting to the matter that is around it. It is then directed toward the gaseous matter target at the end of the tube, the matter and anti-matter collide and annihilate, totally converting to energy. The heat from the reaction is converted to electrical energy in a near 100 percent efficient thermoelectrical generator. This is a device that converts heat directly into electrical energy. Many of our satellites use thermoelectrical generators but their efficiency is very, very low.

All of these actions and reactions are orchestrated perfectly like a tiny little ballet, and in this manner the reactor provides an enormous amount of power.

So back to our original question. What is the power source that provides the power required for this type of travel?

The power source is a reactor that uses element 115 as a fuel, which is totally annihilated to provide the heat which converts to energy, making it a compact, lightweight, efficient onboard power source.

I have got a couple of quick comments about element 115 for those of you who are interested. By virtue of the way it is used in the reactor it depletes very slowly, only 223 grams of 115, which is just under a half a pound, and it can be utilized for a period of twenty to thirty years.

So we have learned how space-time is distorted by a gravitational field, we have learned how a gravitational field is generated, and we have also learned where we get the power to accomplish all of this.

Now it is time to link all of this we have learned in our science lesson to the vehicle that utilizes all this technology. A few years ago I never thought I would hear myself say this, but that vehicle is a disc, which is generally referred to as a flying saucer. I had a partial view of nine different discs at Area S4, but the one I am going to describe to you now is the one that I not only saw two of the three interior levels, but I also saw it fully functional in flight. And, no, unfortunately I didn't get to go for a ride in it.

This particular disc appeared to be in excellent condition, and because of its sleek appearance I nicknamed it the sports model. The sports model was about 16 feet tall and 40 feet in diameter. The exterior skin of this disc is metal which is the color of unpolished stainless steel.

The sports model sits on its belly when it is not energized. As you can see, the hatch is located on the upper part of the disc with the lower portion wrapping around the center lip of the disc. The interior of the disc is divided into three levels. The lower level is where the three gravity amplifiers and guides are located. These are the things that are used to amplify and focus the gravity A wave that we learned about in our science lesson. The reactor is located directly above the three gravity amplifiers on the center level and is, in fact, centered between them. The reactor is similar to the drawing. The element 115 is machined into triangles and inserted into the reactor. This piece of element 115 is the source of the gravity A wave and is the target that is bombarded with protons to release the antimatter, both of which we learned about in our science lesson. The center level of this disc also contains a control panel and seats, both of which were too small and too low to the floor to be functional for adult human beings. The walls in the center level were all divided into archways. At one point in time, when the disc was energized, one of the archways became transparent and you could see the area outside of it, just as if the archway was a window. After the window had been transparent for awhile, a form of writing, which was unlike any alphabetical or scientific or mathematical symbols I had ever seen, began to appear on the transparent archway. I was never informed as to how all of this was achieved, not that any of it would have required alien technology. I was never given access to the upper level of the disc, so I can't enlighten you as to what the portholes are, except that I can assure you that they are not portholes. Now, before I go any further about the disc, I am going to show you where and under what circumstances I saw it tested. My job in this program was to be a part of a back engineering team. Back engineering is the act of taking a finished product and tearing it apart to find out what makes it tick. The goal of this program was to see if the technology of the disc could be duplicated with our material.

When I went to work, I was flown from McCaren Airport in Las Vegas to Area 51, which is a highly secure government area on the Nevada test site. Area 51 is located about 125 miles north of Las Vegas near the Groom Mountains and the Groom dry lake bed. From area 51, I was bussed to an even more highly secure facility, located about 15 miles south of area 51, called S4. S4 is situated at the base of the Papoose Mountains by the Papoose dry lake bed. The air space around S4 is restricted and if any unwelcome aircraft strays into the outer area, they radio the pilot and instruct him or her to leave. If that pilot continues into the middle sector, jets will be scrambled to escort the intruding aircraft out. If, for any reason whatsoever, that aircraft penetrates the inside section before jets can be airborne, ground-to-air missiles will neutralize the intruder.

The moral of this story is: don't try to fly into S4. The S4 installation is built into the mountains and there are nine hangar doors, which are angled at 60 degrees. These doors are covered with a sand-textured coating to blend in with the side of the mountain and the desert floor.

My I.D. badge had a white background with one light blue and one dark blue diagonal strip in the upper lefthand corner. At the bottom of the badge it had numbers and letters indicating various areas including S4. On my badge there was a star punched through S4.

The hangar that housed the sports model was like a typical airplane hangar with the exception of the angled doors, that I mentioned before. The hangar was equipped with typical tools and extensive electronic equipment. It had a machine with an X-ray emblem on it, an overhead crane rated at 20,000 pounds. Equipment in this hangar was marked with a black number 41 with a white circle around it.

It was outside of this hangar that I saw the sports model tested. Now, when a disc is near another source of gravity such as a planet or a moon, it doesn't use the same mode of travel that we learned about in our science lesson. When a disc is near another source of gravity like Earth, the gravity A wave would propagate outward from the disc and its phase shifted into the gravity B wave, which propagates outward from the Earth and this creates lift.

The gravity amplifiers of the disc can be focused independently and they are pulsed, so they don't stay on continuously. When all three of these amplifiers are being used for travel they are in the delta configuration, and when only one is being used for travel, they are in the omicron configuration.

As the intensity of the gravitational field around the disc increases, the distortion of space-time around the disc also increases. If you could see the space-time distortion this is how it would look. As the space-time around the disc increases, it folds over the top of the disc. Looking at the disc from the top, the space-time distortion would be in the shape of a donut. When the disc reaches maximum distortion, it is invisible. This explains how they can suddenly disappear.

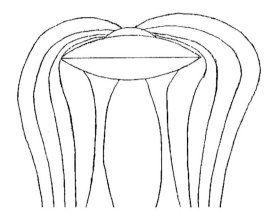

Edward "Billy" Meier has taken an 8 mm film (which has proven to be authentic) in which a disc suddenly blinks out and then, after a short period of time, suddenly blinks back on.

On one occasion, Billy Meier had taken friends with him on one of his many contacts with a spaceship. The friends were required to stand in a separate place from Billy; the spaceship revealed itself to Billy Meier and yet stayed invisible to his friends. The spaceship apparently had the ability to control space-time distortion directionally.

The following is taken from an interview of Bob Lazar from a videotape titled "Secrets of the Black World."

When, at Area S4, I first saw a disc, I thought that it was one of ours, and I thought to myself, well, this explains all of the UFO sightings.

It was actually the second time when I saw the craft, and I got to enter it and look it over. I finally realized what was going on, and that this was an alien craft, and that was a totally different feeling. It was not a feeling of excitement; it was almost an ominous feeling, a feeling as if you shouldn't even be there. It's difficult to describe.

He was asked, what did it look like?

It looked like, if anyone is familiar with Billy Meier sightings, very astonishly similar to that craft. It was very sleek, flying-saucer shaped.

He was asked, did you see the craft in flight?

Bob said, yes, he had seen several flights, but they were short, low altitude flights. But they were not out of the atmosphere, because they have a prize possession here and they are not going to risk taking a chance of losing it.

I witnessed several test flights outside the compound, and also saw one at probably one hundred feet away.

He was asked, what was the sound when it was in flight?

Bob replied that it was very quiet, and with a slight hissing sound. There was also a slight blue glow from the bottom, probably due to the extreme voltage that was present on the craft. After it rose the blue glow disappeared and then just gently glided and later set down.

New government misinformation about extraterrestrial space travel was put forth on Peter Jenning's two-hour UFO program on ABC, February 24, 2005. Of course, we know from Bob Lazar's science lesson that the U.S. government knows that hyper-space travel is accomplished by warping space-time with gravity. On this program they said that Einstein had stated that you could not go faster than the speed of light, but there was a possibility that extraterrestrial space travel could be accomplished through wormholes.

In fact, I doubt their statement that Einstein said that nothing could go faster than the speed of light. If you read the part earlier, you will find that Einstein, in 1915, solved the orbit problem of Mercury by proving that the Sun's gravity was warping space-time, which produced a non-Newtonian warp in the trajectory of Mercury.

Crash and Retrieval Records

According to Bob Lazar and several others, there are, at Area S4, nine hangers built into the base of the mountain. The hanger doors are on a 60 degree angle and covered with a sand textured finish to blend in with the desert. Bob Lazar and others have reported that there are from seven to nine extraterrestrial space ships in these hangers.

In the following pages I am going to tell how I believe seven of these space ships got to be in the hangers.

ARIZONA

1   Behind the Flying Saucers, The first downed Saucer was in a very rocky high plateau, east of Aztec, New Mexico. 100 feet in diameter, 16 bodies.

2   Behind the Flying Saucers, the second one landed near the Yuma Proving ground west of Phoenix. It was 72 feet in diameter and had 16 dead bodies.

3   Behind the flying Saucers, the third ship came down right above Phoenix, in Paradise Valley. It was 36 feet in diameter, two dead bodies.

NEW MEXICO

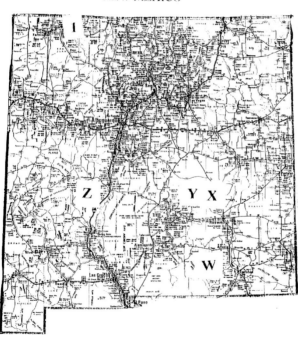

W   Jim Ragsdale had lived much of his entire life in fear of threats on his life because of a space ship crash that he and a girl friend witnessed when on a camping trip to the Lincoln National Forest, which is some 58 miles south and west of Roswell.

When dying of cancer and on his death bed he finally told the story. On the Fourth of July weekend in 1947, Jim Ragsdale made plans to take a girl friend to the Lincoln National Forest camp grounds. He left Carlsbad, where he worked and drove up Pine Lodge Road. At mile marker 53 he turned south for four or five miles, drove past the water pipe and found an isolated area where he and his girl friend could have complete privacy.

Jim and his girlfriend were sleeping in his camper pickup, about midnight they saw a flash which was intense and they heard a noise that sounded like thunder, and then shortly after that they saw this bright light that was coming towards them from the north, a few moments later they saw an object trailing flame. They were afraid the object was going to crash right on them. They saw the object clip the pine trees right off, hit the ground and wedge between two big rocks.

Jim was able to climb into the space craft and to view the bodies. He said the bodies were not human-like. He was very interested in how it was put together and how it worked, because there was no engine and it was unlike anything he had ever seen.

X   Information from SHOWTIME video cassette, 9-31-94. While the Army was picking up every little scrap of debris from Mac Brazel's ranch, there were two small surveillance airplanes checking the area. They found a bell shaped space ship at the base of a cliff, 2 1/2 miles east of the debris area. 3 to 6 bodies.

Y   Frank Kaufman – The night of July 4th, 1947 about 11:00 p.m. – radar showed something went down east of White Sands – and north of Roswell – people driving on U.S. 285 north going south noticed an orange ball falling toward Earth. MPs were sent out on 285 to locate where this orange ball fell to Earth. It was about 15 miles off the highway.

Z   Barney Barnett, a resident of Sororro, New Mexico, a civil engineer working for the Federal Government in soil conservation, was one of the first witnesses to arrive at the site of a fallen saucer, sometime in the morning of July 3, 1947.

This is what Barney said to his friend L.W. "Vern" Matlais and his wife, Jean Swedmark Maltais.

I was out on assignment, near Magdalena, which is close to the Plains of San Agustin, one morning when the light reflecting off of some sort of large metallic object caught my eye. Thinking that a plane might have crashed during the night, I went over to where it was—about a mile, perhaps a mile and a quarter away on flat desert land. By the time I got there, I realized that it wasn't a plane at all, but some sort of metallic, disc-shaped object about twenty five or thirty feet across. While I was looking at it and trying to decide what it was, some other people came up from the other direction and began looking around too. They told me later that they were part of an archaeological research team from some eastern university (the University of Pennsylvania) and that they too had thought that a plane had crashed. They were all over the place looking at the wreck.

I noticed that they were standing around looking at some dead bodies that had fallen to the ground. I think there were others (dead bodies) in the machine, which was a sort of metallic instrument of some sort – a kind of disc. It was not all that big. It seemed to be made of metal that looked like dirty stainless steel. The machine had been split open by an explosion or impact.

I tried to get close to see what the bodies were like. They were all dead as far as I could see and there were bodies inside and outside the vehicle. They were like humans but they were not humans. The heads were round, the eyes were small, and they had no hair. The eyes were oddly spaced. They were quite small by our standards and their heads were larger in proportion to their bodies than ours. Their clothing seemed to be one-piece and gray in color. You couldn't see any zippers, belts, or buttons. They seemed to me to be all males. I was close enough to touch them but I didn't – I was escorted away before I could look at them anymore.

While we were looking at them a military officer drove up in a truck with a driver and took control. He told everybody that the Army was taking over and to get out of the way. Other military personnel came up and cordoned off the area. We were told to leave the area and not to talk to anyone whatever about what we had seen… that it was our patriotic duty to remain silent….

Abductions

Chapter 1
A Partial Summary

There is no such thing as a complete summary of abductions. There have been literally thousands, and possibly hundreds of thousands, of abductions, and I am going to summarize a few of the most famous, or at least the most written about abduction cases, and some of their identifying features.

Barney and Betty Hill

Nineteen sixty-one in the White Mountains, New Hampshire. Barney and Betty Hill were driving late at night when they saw a light that gradually approached their car and then slowed to a stop. They pulled off the main road for a closer look. The lighted object hovered low enough for them to see that it was a structured craft of unusual shape. Using binoculars, Barney Hill was able to make out the ship's occupants looking back at him through a row of windows. A moment or two later their conscious recollections of this event ended. The next thing they knew they were driving along the original route and became aware that they had somehow lost two hours. In the days and weeks that followed, Barney Hill began to suffer from extreme anxiety, insomnia, and nightmares. Eventually he developed an ulcer and his condition worsened. He sought medical and psychiatric help. His psychiatrist, Dr. Benjamin Simon, felt that he had some kind of unremembered trauma, and therefore began a series of hypnotic regressions to uncover and cure the problem. It was in this context that Barney Hill recalled what had happened during the missing two hours. The UFO had landed that night and he had been paralyzed and then taken onboard along with his wife. Separately they had been subjected to some sort of physical examination. Dr. Simon had regularly given Barney the post-hypnotic suggestion that he would not remember the material recovered during hypnosis once the trance had ended. When Betty Hill was later regressed, she knew nothing of her husband's recollections, so her congruent descriptions of the craft, its interior, and its occupants were extremely important. Today it can be seen as a watershed case event in the abduction phenomenon.

Budd Hopkins is without a doubt THE foremost authority in the world on UFO abductions. He has written three books on the subject, MISSING TIME, INTRUDERS, and WITNESSED.

I will summarize the later two, however, before I do that I need to mention two other giants in the Abduction field.

David M. Jacobs, associate professor of history at Temple University, has written five books on the subject of UFOs and Abductions.

John E. Mack, M.D. is a professor of psychiatry at the Cambridge Hospital, Harvard Medical School, and founding director of the Center of Psychology and Social Change. He wrote the Pulitzer Prize winning book A Prince of Our Disorder. His book, "Abduction" makes an important contribution to the subject.

Intruders

The list of characters
Kathy Davis – mother of two boys
Rob – 4 years old
Tommie – 3 years old
Her Mother
Laura – Kathy's sister

The setting
Copley Woods

The neighborhood itself is normally peaceful and pleasant, a typical middle-western, middle-class suburbia. The houses have enough distance between them to allow natural privacy and isolation, and the area is just far enough away from downtown Indianapolis to suggest an almost rural environment. The Davis family owns three acres of land in the Copley Woods and lives quite comfortably with an impressive array of automobiles, kitchen appliances, television sets, and backyard swimming pools. Robert Davis is a good provider. He is a highly skilled technical person that is well compensated. Besides Robert four others live in the Davis house: His wife Mary; their daughter Kathy, a divorcee; and her two children Robby and Tommy. In September of 1983 I received a letter from Kathy Davis, which triggered a two and half year investigation into events in and around the Copley Woods.

When Budd opened the letter some fifteen colored photographs spilled out. He recognized immediately the familiar image of a UFO landing trace, a circular area of ground in which all the grass appears to be dead, as if it has been subject to heat or some other form of radiation.

Kathy began her letter by explaining that there were two things she wanted to inform Budd about. The event documented in the photographs and a "missing time" incident that occurred years before, involving her older sister. She wrote first about the more recent incident.

...Around the first week of July, 1983, about 8:00 to 9:00 P.M., I was preparing to go out and sew a little at a neighbor's home. And while I was standing at the kitchen window I noticed a light in the pool house and the door was open. I remembered shutting it earlier, so I knew it shouldn't be open, let alone have a light on, so I mentioned it to mom. She looked and wondered what was up, but neither one of us were all that alarmed. When I got ready to leave, I decided to drive around the turn-around to make sure that no one was out there, as mom would be alone with the kids (Rob, 4, and Tommy, 3). When I did the light was off and the door was shut, and the garage door was open (which is always kept shut). When I got to Dee Annes house (one street over) I called mom and told her what I saw and asked if she would like me to come home and check it out, and she sounded rather nervous (not at all like my mom). She said that she had seen a big light by the pool house, and it moved up to the bird feeder and grew to about two feet in diameter. But she didn't see any beam. It was just like a spot light on the bird feeder, nothing else around it. When I got there it was gone, and I looked around the property (with my dad's 22, I'm chicken). I did finally find my dog Penny hiding under a car out back. Usually she carries on something fierce when anyone she doesn't know comes on the property. It's not like her to hide and have to be coaxed out from anywhere, especially by me. She's usually all over me. I didn't see anything, so went back to sew and later that night, Dee and I and her daughter came back about midnight and went swimming. Right after that night our yard was burned, by what we don't know. Nothing will grow there now, at first Penny would walk half way around the yard to avoid walking on it. Birds will no longer go near the bird feeder either, and we have always had tons of birds every day, especially red birds. Well that is the story of our back yard mystery. Its still here for anyone who wants to see it.

Now about Laura. My sister Laura is thirty-five years old. She has always been level-headed and not very imaginative. Always the realist. In the summer of 1965, she left one evening about 4:30 P.M. to take my mother to play bingo. On the way home from dropping her off, as she was passing the church on 10th Street, she was suddenly compelled to pull into the church parking lot around back. [As Budd explains later in the book, this is a fairly common happening and there is no doubt that the UFO occupants have the ability to cause this to happen.] She noticed that there weren't any cars around and thought it quite strange for a Sunday afternoon in that busy area. When she parked she looked and saw something she had never seen before. It was silver and I believe she said the lights were red, green, and white, flashing somewhat (flickering might be a better word). It was hovering soundlessly...over the lot about telephone pole high, right over her car. All she remembers now is she reached over to turn down her radio to see if it made noise. Then the next thing she remembers is it's dark out and she looks up and this thing is gone and she is driving down the street. When she went to get mom that night they drove around looking for it, but never saw anything else. [Budd explains that with the sightings of the UFO and the obvious missing time, because of the sudden darkness, Laura was abducted.]

Having finished her account of the mysterious backyard lights, the marks on the ground, and her sister's UFO experiences, Kathie added the final cryptic paragraph.

My mother and I have had a couple of unusual experiences, mine mostly in the form of vivid dreams, and mother and I both have the same scars on our right legs. She got hers when she was a little girl playing outside. I don't remember when I got mine, but it seems like I've had it all my life. They are in the same place and look exactly alike. A nurse once told me it looked like a scar left by a bone marrow test or a pin inserted in my shin bone from a break. At first I only had one scar, but now I have two—on the same leg about 3-_ inches apart. I got this one when I was about 13, but I can't for the life of me remember how. I used to play in the woods by the pond a lot, and I may have gotten it there, but I don't remember how.

Usually when Budd received a letter in response to *Missing Time* they were read and then stacked in a cardboard box to be answered later when time permitted, a batch at a time. If the tone of the letter sounded urgent and it suggested a buried abduction experience, he often phoned the writer directly. The "Kathie case" fit this special category. He called for the first time on September 15, 1983. A number of home conversations ensued, leading up to arrangement for Kathie to visit New York in the middle of October for an intensified investigation of her experiences and a series of hypnotic regressions.

During these phone calls I talked with Kathie, her mother, her father, and her sister Laura. One of my first conversations was with Kathie's father, Robert. I asked him his recollections of the circle and patch of dead grass that had appeared on the lawn behind the house.

"Well, I have been working on this damn yard out there, and the backyard was the best part of the whole place. I don't know what did it. Its not a fungus. I don't know what the devil it is, but something or some-one or whatever has wiped out a hunk of my damn ground. The circle and that line away from it are still just like they were, and they've been there about three months. They haven't changed at all; the grass just grows up to the circle and quits."

Robert, Mary, and Kathie all agree that it took perhaps three days for the grass to die and then crumble away to a brown powder. The marks were unmistakable by the Fourth of July, when Mary remembered point-ing them out to her grandson. Shrubbery near the bird feeder, where Mary had first seen the small ball of light, began to die also.

For Kathie the most unforgettable experience occurred in the summer of 1978, when she was nineteen years old, newly married, and living with her husband in a small attic apartment in a suburb of Indianapolis.

The dream was extraordinarily frightening and realistic, Kathie recalled, an experience as vivid now as it had been then. It began in the middle of the night with Kathie sitting up, awake, facing two strange, gray-faced creatures who stood alongside her bed. One of them was holding a small black box with a glistening red light on its top. The "man" who held the box moved closer and handed it to Kathie, and as he moved the other figure moved too in absolute unison. In an account she wrote later she described it this way: "When they handed me the box I remembered thinking, 'Oh, please don't come any closer!' Just as I wrote that I felt the terror, and it all felt too real. The feeling, the dream! For just a flash I thought this could be real. I don't know. The terror is real!"

She described the figures as having large heads and skin that was "dingy white, almost gray." Their eyes were "pitch black in color, liquid like, shimmering in the dim light." She mentioned that she could not remember seeing a hand when the box was passed to her and that the figures were so close to the bed that she could not see their lower legs or feet.

"I don't remember if there was a mouth or nose or ears. I just remember the eyes best and the general shape. They were between four and five feet tall, I guess, and slight of build. He called me by name and talked to me like I was a child. I don't know why I feel this; it didn't seem to bother me.

"I was scared, petrified, but as soon as I heard my name and looked at his face, his eyes, I could calm down enough to communicate. I felt more physically relaxed, almost sleepy again, and quieter mentally. I just kept thinking, *Just don't come any closer and don't touch me! Don't move closer to me, please!* They never touched me and they moved slowly, cautiously. I never saw them leave; I just woke up."

Kathie said that this "dream" seemed utterly real. She was in her own bedroom, and everything appeared exactly as it normally was except for the presence of the strange visitors. Her husband was asleep beside her through the entire ordeal, yet she made no effort to alert him. At about three A.M. she awoke slowly, as if from an anesthetic, as she put it, and roused her husband to tell him of her bizarre recollection. The following day she told her mother as well as her sister Laura. Budd has since interviewed both women as well as Kathie's ex-husband on this point, and all three recall Kathie's having told them at that time (1978) of her frightening "dream." All the details pre-date the publication of his book *Missing Time*. (She also did not see the film *Close Encounters of the Third Kind*, until her father took the whole family to see it a year later at Christmastime.) I am satisfied that in 1978 she had almost no knowledge of the typical "bedroom visitation" nor of this commonly reported UFO occupant type.

On Budd's third phone conversation with Kathie, he asked if she herself had ever seen anything she took to be an actual UFO, as to opposed to the odd light in the pool shed or the two strange figures in her "dream." She answered somewhat hesitantly that she and two other teenagers had several times seen odd moving lights late at night when they were driving around, in Kathie's phrase, "out in the boonies." Budd asked for details.

"My friend Dorothy and I sometimes cruised around spying on Dorothy's boyfriend," Kathie recalled. We always seemed to have a good time but we don't remember what we did. But one time I remember we saw this weird light. It was flashing like a strobe. I said, 'Hey, look at that light up there.' Then somebody said it was a UFO, and we all started giggling. And then it got closer. And then it got closer. And it started flashing. We all got a creepy feeling. I was more fascinated than I was scared. I remember we stopped the car to look at it."

Kathie's memories at this point became vague, so Budd asked her to visit her friend Dorothy and find out what she remembered about that night. The next day Kathie called him. "I was really surprised," she said. "When I got Dorothy on the phone, I told her you wanted to know what she remembered about the time we saw the flashing light and stopped the car. She said, 'Do you mean the light in the sky or the light on the ground that we got out to look at?' Now the strange thing is I don't remember seeing any light on the ground. I barely remember getting out of the car. I don't remember anything else about it at all, except that Roberta was hiding on the floor in the backseat, scared to death and wanting to go home. The whole thing was peculiar. I remember I spent the night at Dorothy's, and that we had barely gotten into bed when her parents' alarm went off and it was time for them to go to work. I know it was almost dawn when we came in, but I can't for the life of me remember what we did all that time. Dorothy doesn't know what we did either, but she remembers how late it was." Then Kathie, recognizing the irony of the situation, chuckled and said, "I remember one of us saying 'time really flies when you are having fun.'"

As the reader will learn, Kathie's conscious recollections of that night concealed an extremely harrowing UFO abduction experience, an event of crucial importance for our understanding of the UFO phenomenon.

One of the requests I made of Kathie and her family was that they carefully look over the ground behind their house near the burned area and look for any marks or disturbances that they may not have noticed before. I also asked for samples of the soil from the undisturbed ground immediately adjacent to it. By going back to her appointment book, Kathie had been able to fix the date of the backyard events—the lights, the armed search, her mother's account of the illuminated bird feeder, etc.—as having been June 30, 1983. So my request for soil samples came two and a half months after the event. I knew, therefore, that any evidential weight the samples might have had was now probably compromised. But Kathie's search at the burned circle yielded an important new find: About two feet out from the eight-foot-diameter circle, equidistant from the center and from each other, were four small holes, finger-thick and about three inches deep. These small holes, which could easily have been made by some sort of fixed, symmetrical landing gear, have their precedent in other similar UFO cases.

Seven years before, I had investigated the first of scores of UFO reports that turned out to involve an abduction and which established a by now familiar pattern. In that first case a young man, Steve Kilburn, was immobilized after his automobile was pulled off the road as if by some powerful external force. He was then approached by five grayish, large-headed humanoid figures. Like Kathie and so many other abductees, Kilburn's attention was drawn almost hypnotically to his captor's eyes, which he describes as "really shiny...black, I don't see any pupils or anything...and they are big...they're black and endless. Like they are liquid or something...I keep looking at these eyes looking at me. God, I feel like I am under a microscope."

It is worth noting that in Kathie's 1978 "dream," she also described the small, gray-skinned figure's eyes as "pitch black in color, liquid-like, shimmering in the dim light. When I looked at his face, his eyes, I calmed down enough to communicate."

Kilburn was taken inside the UFO and placed upon a table where he underwent an intermittently painful examination that included the taking of a sperm sample. Later he was returned to his car and the memory of this traumatic encounter was somehow temporarily blocked.

Since the Kilburn case I have worked directly with over one hundred people who apparently have had the same kind of UFO abduction experience. These individuals, it should be pointed out, come from every educational, social, and economic level of our society. I have investigated the cases of three different abductees who hold Ph.D. degrees. Other abductees I've worked with include a psychotherapist, a police officer, a lawyer for the United States government, a farmer, an army officer, a business executive, a well-known writer, an artist, a registered nurse, and so on.

Because the abduction history of the Davis family is so complicated and the details so numerous I am going to list the UFO incidents in outline form.

1.   Probably the winter of 1966, when Kathie was seven years old. Kathie and her sister Laura visit family friends, who have moved to the Detroit area. Kathie goes outside to play, and after a flash of light and a loud noise she wanders off. She becomes lost but sees what appears to her as her friend's house. Though it is cold and there is snow on the ground, the door to the house is open. She enters and meets a strange looking family; a "little boy" takes her into his "playroom," a round white windowless place, where she is asked to sit down on the floor. "I am going to play a trick on you," he says, and a small machine-like device makes a sudden sharp cut on her lower leg. For a moment the little boy metamorphoses into a small large-headed gray-skinned figure standing by a table. After an unremembered interim, she is put out of this "house" by the odd family. Still lost, she sees her sister Laura approaching, walking as if asleep. Without a word Laura takes her hand, turns around, and they return to their friend's house. The larger of Kathie's two scars, the upper one, is the result of this experience.

2.   July 1975. Rough River State Park, Kentucky. Kathie, sixteen years old, visits the park with her seventeen-year-old friend Nan and others. After sighting four spiraling lights, Kathie encounters a normal-looking man and his two tall, silent companions who behave oddly. (The normal-looking man was a brownish-blond and looked similar to the ones in the Travis Walton story.)

3.   December 1977. Indianapolis, Indiana. In a rural area, eighteen-year-old Kathie and her friends Dorothy and Roberta are driving late at night. An oddly flashing light is sighted, which eventually comes down to the ground. Dorothy stops the car to investigate while a frightened Roberta cowers in the backseat. Kathie is taken into a landed UFO and undergoes a gynecological operation.

4.   March 1978. At her sister Laura's house outside Indianapolis, Kathie is abducted and taken into a UFO where a second gynecological operation occurs.

5.   Spring or summer 1979. While pregnant with Robbie, Kathie is taken from her Indianapolis apartment into a UFO. While lying upon a table she experiences, among other things, the sensation of thin probes being pressed up into her nostrils. She is shown a small black box and is told that she will remember what it's for.

6.   1980. Kathie receives a series of enigmatic, indecipherable phone calls at regular intervals during the nine months of her pregnancy with

Tommy. No hypnosis has been attempted with respect to these strange calls, and they remain unexplored.

7. June 30, 1983. A UFO lands near her parents' house and Kathie is immobilized and irradiated with light. A probe is inserted in her ear, and she suffers what seems to be the effect of mild radiation poisoning. This incident triggered her initial letter.

8. October 3, 1983. Kathie undergoes a two-stage abduction. While driving to the store, her car is stopped and a conversation takes place with a small gray-skinned figure. A little later she is taken from her bedroom and moved into a UFO. After a physical examination of some sort she is shown a small child. Details of the abduction's two stages emerged in two hypnotic sessions, widely separated in time. The earlier details surfaced in October of 1983 shortly after the incident's occurrence. Kathie's recollections of the child only came to light months later, spontaneously, without the use of hypnosis; in fact, hypnosis was not employed to flesh out these later recollections of the little girl.

9. November 26, 1983. The Davis house is entered by a small large-headed figure who paralyzes Robbie while apparently placing a nasal implant into little Tommy. Kathie meanwhile is re-abducted. Hypnosis on Kathie's apparently simultaneous abduction was not carried out until May 1986.

10. February 1986. Kathie is awakened by Robbie, who describes being frightened by a red light gliding "like a spider" down his wall. Minutes later, Kathie sees a small gray-skinned figure walk calmly past her door after apparently having emerged from the bedroom where Tommie was sleeping by himself. This incident was not explored by hypnosis.

11. April 1986. Kathie is abducted again from the Davis home and is shown a tiny baby. The way Kathie handles the tiny infant is carefully observed.

12. September 1986. Kathie, while driving to her apartment late at night with Robbie and Tommy in the car, at two different times and locations, see a large, glowing oval object hovering over the treetops. Unaccountably she arrives over one hour late. Several hours later Robbie comes into her room suffering from a serious nosebleed—his very first. As of this writing the events of that evening have not been explored, but the account suggests that one more abduction may have occurred, one that was possibly focused on Robbie instead of his brother and which may have involved a nasal implant.

Chapter 2
An Overview of Budd Hopkin's Book: *Witnessed*

In contrast to the secret way the aliens operated in Budd Hopkins's book, *Intruders*, and all other abduction happenings, the following display of the aliens' technology was done because of the following four listed objects, one of them being Budd Hopkins himself. It shows that the aliens wanted the whole world to know what they could do. The reason why seems to be rather ambiguous, but then everything about the small gray-skinned creatures with the large, black, controlling eyes seems to be ambiguous.

No. 1—Budd Hopkins, the foremost authority in the world on UFO abductions, who lives in New York

No. 2—New York, the world's most renowned city

No. 3—The world headquarters for the United Nations

No. 4—The Brooklyn Bridge, a world renowned landmark

The main character, Linda Cortile (a fictitious name given to her by Budd Hopkins), was already known by Budd Hopkins because Linda had called him in the spring of 1989. The reason she had called was because of Budd's book *Intruders* and because of UFO abduction experiences she had in her youth and childhood. On November 30, 1989, she telephoned him about an incident she had the night before. A little after 3:00 A.M., as she was about to fall asleep, she noticed a feeling of numbness creeping up her legs and sensed a strange presence in the room. With a sudden pang of fear she saw a diminutive, large-headed figure with enormous black eyes moving toward her. Her memories after that point became cloudy and fragmentary, but felt she had been floated out of her living room window and lifted up into a hovering UFO. The Cortile family lives on the twelfth floor of an apartment building in downtown Manhattan, near Catherine Street and only two blocks from FDR Drive and the Brooklyn Bridge.

Now remember, at this point in time Budd Hopkins only knew that Linda Cortile suspected that she had been floated out of her living room window (which was closed) into a hovering UFO.

Budd Hopkins received a letter, which was postmarked February 1, 1991. This was fourteen months after Linda's suspected ordeal.

This is a synopsis of what it said, with corrections in brackets.

Dear Mr. Hopkins,
My partner and I are police officers. [This is not true. They were actually some type of U.S. government secret servicemen, and they were driving a limousine and had a passenger who was a foreign representative to the United Nations.] We have been in a serious dilemma because of our strict profession and our lack of knowledge on this subject.

We didn't know what to do or who to turn to and hadn't done so until recently. We searched the bookstores over and came up with you. There was an address in your book *Intruders*, but it was through your publishers. In turn we let our fingers do the walking through the white pages. Much to our surprise, there you were. We're hoping that you are the correct Budd Hopkins.

So here it goes...

One early morning, about three or three-thirty A.M. in late November 1989, we sat in our patrol car [limousine] underneath the elevated FDR Drive on South Catherine Slip, observing the surroundings ahead. [Actually their limousine went dead along with their radio communications. This happened because a UFO wanted them stopped to be able to see the following scene.] Sitting on the passenger side of our vehicle, I reached into my shirt pocket for a stick of gum. As I opened it, I looked down at the silver wrapping that was left in my hand and saw it reflecting a firelight type of reddish glow. I looked up through the windshield to see where it was coming from and there it was—a strange oval hovering over the top of an apartment building, two to three blocks up from where we were sitting. We don't know where it came from.

Its lights turned from a bright reddish orange to a very whitish blue, coming out from the bottom of it. It moved out away from the building and lowered itself to an apartment window just below. I yelled for my partner, who was sitting beside me, behind the wheel of the patrol car [limousine] and he was just as excited as I was. I had to be sure

77

of what I was seeing, so I went into the glove compartment to get a pair of binoculars. We grabbed a hold of each other and were going to get out of the car, but what could we do for that poor little girl or woman wearing a full white nightgown? She was floating in midair in a bright beam of whitish blue light, looking like an angel. She was then brought up into the bottom of that very large oval (about three quarters the size of the building across).

This poor person was escorted out of her window. I don't know if she was willing or not. I don't think so because it seemed as though she was being escorted up into this thing by three ugly but smaller human-like creatures, one above her and two below. They seemed to be in charge. On top of our fear of getting involved, we were also carrying a load of guilt because we didn't help her and we don't know what became of her.

After she was escorted up and in, the oval turned reddish orange again and whisked away, coming in our direction, above us. It must have flown over the FDR Drive while we were sitting underneath it. It then plunged into the river behind us, not far from pier 17, behind the Brooklyn Bridge. Someone else had to see what happened that morning. I know what we saw and we'll never forget it.

Mr. Hopkins, the oval never came up from under the river. It's possible that it could have after we drove away about 45 minutes later. We could have stayed longer, but we couldn't ignore our radio any longer.

After that the story gets more and more complicated. However, the point I want to make is that this whole episode basically happened because of the four preceding points I made at the beginning. The odds of this happening by chance are astronomical!

In other words, this whole show was totally under the control of the aliens, and they wanted the whole world to know.

For the purpose of my book I am going to end this part of "Abductions" here. However, this book *Witnessed* is a very interesting, complicated, and an unbelievable book and should be read in its entirety.

The Billy Meier Story
Switzerland

The following was taken from a videotape titled "The Meier's Chronicles." This tape was produced in 1986 by four people, Lee and Britt Elders, Tom Welch, and Wendel Stevens, by a company called Intercept from Phoenix, Arizona.

This interview took place around a large table in Billy Meier's house. The interviewers were Lee and Britt Elders, Tom Welch, Wendel Stevens, and the unknown man with the microphone (he appeared to be Asian). Also present were Billy Meier, the man to be interviewed, and his wife Kaliope.

Billy Meier has been asked, what is the reason the Pleiadians are here?

In his answer Billy uses the word "naturalism." The dictionary's first definition for naturalism is: action, inclination, or thought based only on natural desires and instincts.

This is Billy Meier's answer: "There are two points, and they are very important. The naturalism way and the spiritual way. They have to work together, not only one of them has to work, and to change this to the real way, to the collective way."

They came here *again* to teach Earth people. That is the only reason they had.

The First Contact

It was Tuesday, 28 January 1975, at 13:00, when I was occupied at home with trying to record "tape-voices," a try that had been unsuccessful for months and also continued further on. Nevertheless, on that day I was lucky, even if it was other than what I expected. It concerned something for this point in time completely new and pertained to an event I had not expected until one year later.

It was as if it were from out of nothing, which allowed me to listen inside. Slowly all became clear for me, and for the first time resolved matters were slowly crystallizing themselves. They were words, thoughts of someone, which slowly made themselves understandable to me and allowed me to listen. They were very peaceful and very familiar to me, though they came up in this strange manner and forced themselves into me. And they came to me from someone who was, up to now, unknown to me. Quite suddenly I understood the meaning of these symbolic picture forms and words that transmitted a message to me that I should take a camera and leave the house. I did this without questioning and without knowing why I did so; it was like obeying an irresistible command. The call seemed to be for me, almost like soft coercion. So I took my vehicle, a motorcycle, and drove away. I drove aimlessly, it seemed to me, but well guided to a certain place, as later became evident.

I drove through the village (Hinwil) on several streets, and some ten minutes beyond. I came to fields, drove across and along through meadows and forests, and in this way reached a quiet lonely area (in the Frecht Nature Reserve). On a little road, near the nature preserve region, stood a long distance transport truck whose driver had disappeared into the near forest, apparently to do something. Interested in the big van, I stopped and examined it from all sides. It was a German truck judging by the control number on the plates.

I glanced at my watch and noticed that it was 14:12. I had been driving around for a full hour already. Just at this moment, I heard a very silent but somehow known, peculiar stirring in the air, so I looked up into the cloudy sky. What I saw made me wonder if I was dreaming, though this sight was already known to me since earliest youth. Yet what I saw was not expected so soon. As I had been told, I counted on this first happening one year later, still to come.

From out of the clouds an object came, reducing its speed considerably, and slowly curved along about 350 meters of forest. The stirring had suddenly stopped as the object reduced its speed more. It now flew in complete silence, and I could see its exact form, a disc-like object with similar shape on top and bottom. The upper dome was some larger than the base and was equipped with red, high placed rectangles, if I saw correctly.

Hastily I seized my camera and aimed at the object, because I knew very well from earlier experience that I had to be very quick with the photographing if I wanted to have a chance of having a photo on the film. Because of their extreme velocity, erratic flying, and sudden disappearing, these objects can seldom be photographed, and then in most cases are only seen in pictures as dissolved shadows. So I quickly snapped the first picture, at exactly 14:15, when the object was only 150 meters away from me, and also flying about 150 meters above the ground.

Only a fraction of a second after shooting this picture the object rapidly sped away to the west and disappeared. Then, suddenly stirring, it was in the air again, but the flying object had rapidly returned already and was hovering about 100 meters above the truck. Just as suddenly, the stirring grew silent again. It was exactly 44 meters to the truck as later measured.

It was then that I shot the second picture. But just at the moment I pushed the release on my camera, the object began to approach from that hover position to stop suddenly in the air only 50 meters above the ground beyond the truck. Now I was able to see the object very distinctly and to recognize it as certainly not an Earth flying machine, but an extraterrestrial flight vehicle. At first it was still an unidentified flying object of unknown origin, a flying saucer, as the objects had in error so ridiculously become designated.

The lower side of the disc seemed to vibrate as though it were alive. It looked a little like waves running continuously in and through the underside of the ship, by which the skin appeared damaged and old, nearly like a washing board. These waves seemed to be irregular and inconsistent, but very peculiar and energetic. Solid matter seemed to dissolve in the radiation of the waves. The truck looked like it was suddenly enveloped in heat waves. I could not see it clearly. Besides this, it seemed much farther away than the UFO that hovered only 50 meters behind it, which in fact was not the case.

When I shot the second picture it was exactly 14:18. Then the object sped from its hover position and rapidly ascended toward the east into the sky and disappeared into the clouds. Quickly the newly heard stirring faded away and tranquility returned.

I turned back to my bike, which I had left a bit aside, started the vehicle, and drove across the fields toward the edge of the east woods. There was a very large boggy clearing. About 250 meters farther on I got off my bike in the field and walked along. Sunk in thought and rather disinterested, I now noticed the truck was about 500 meters in the distance and driving away; its driver, meanwhile, must have returned from the forest.

When the truck was gone, in that lonely region no other human being existed except for me, and the voices of nature could be heard. About 200 meters in front of me, there in the clearing, five roes grazed peacefully, while in the forest some ravens high in the birch, fir, and beech trees had a fight with a bird of prey. But they suddenly and unexpectedly left their victim and silently disappeared. At 300 meters distance, a farmer's yard watchdog began to bark like crazy. Flying fast, the ravens disappeared away over the tops of the trees. The five roes too had suddenly become excited, threw up their heads sniffing, and looked around cautiously. From standing still, they suddenly bolted away in great leaps and wide bounds, away from the forest and into the open field. Only a few meters away, they ran past me to a south woods area. Evidently whatever frightened them had disturbed them very much, but it was evident that I was not the cause because they did not care about me in their flight. The sudden driving escape of the ravens now appeared strange to me too, as they normally did not give up so easy, and especially for no reason.

Two or three minutes passed, and then I again heard the now familiar stirring sound. Coming from the east, the object rushed down from the clouds again and slowed its speed very quickly over the woods. The sound died out again, and now I knew the reason for the escape of the ravens and the roes. They had evidently sensed the approach of the object with their finer senses and fled in panic.

Slowly the object curved down over the forest toward the clearing, and now very slowly it sank down there. I now shot the next picture, the third one now, and that was exactly at 14:31. One minute later the fourth picture followed, taken from about 180 meters away. Then I saw the object sink down further to the ground and finally touched gently on the meadow ground of the clearing—completely silent, as the stirring had died away.

After the landing I boldly went up and wanted to observe the object from closeby, but about a 100 meters before the object, a great power seemed to check my progress. It seemed like I was bucking the winds of a silent storm, or against an opposite pole magnet. With a great effort I tried to struggle against this and to move forward. I even succeeded at this but only for a few meters. Then the counteracting force was simply too great, and I just sat down there on the ground. I stared over at the object and waited to see what would happen, surely it would come. I was not mistaken, because in less than a minute something happened—from behind the object a figure appeared, obviously a human being in a peculiar but nevertheless already known to me suit. It was a cosmic suit, something like those that are used by Earth astronauts, except it was not as clumsy and heavy as the Earth product. It seemed to be very pliant and light. Actually the suit was more like a coverall of a peculiar gray color. From very close it looked as if it were made of elephant's skin. At least the material reminded me of the skin of an elephant I once had touched in Africa, and also another whose skin I once touched and looked at closer in the zoo. Besides this, the suit was close-fitted on the body and extremely durable, which was easy to see. Around the neck ran a ring that evidently served for the mounting of a helmet, which this long-haired UFOnaut was not wearing now. Evidently the Earth's atmosphere was suited for her. The head was free and no doubt that of a woman or simply a girl. The look on her face was open and free, and nothing indicated super-humanness, pretentiousness, or spirituality. She just seemed to be a normal human being, without super-ability or super-beauty. She simply looked like a quite normal female creature, though she was devilishly attractive. She also walked like a normal woman, yet somewhat stronger and more sure. She was not particularly dainty, affected, proud, or trying to make any special impression. She just walked like a woman with natural self-consciousness, self-confidence and easy natural grace.

Slowly this creature came near to me, seized me by my arm and pulled me up. The grip of the girl was strong and sure, but yet very pleasant and secure. By slow steps we went to my vehicle, where we both just sat down in the dry grass. Then the UFO-girl began to speak, not in my home language but in a perfect German, with an accent peculiar to me. The introductory conversation was not very long, but the following conversation lasted for a longer time before the girl went off again. She disappeared into the object and flew away, to vanish from my sight seconds later high above the clouds.

She left me at 15:51. Shortly after the starting of the ship, at 15:58, I shot some more pictures from about 185 meters away. With interest, I noticed that shortly before starting the ship, below and to the side of it everything merged together in strong heat waves that seemed to dissolve the environment as well of the contours of the trees and all, while everything changed into different colors, evidently by some radiation. Also the distance seemed to alternate, and everything gave the impression of being distorted, as I had already seen when I snapped the second picture. At the start of the ship it was easier to see, and I noticed the absolute clearness of a blue-red radiation, which may be seen in the fifth exposure.

We learned in the science lesson in the Bob Lazar tape about space-time distortion, which is caused by an intense gravitational field. This is, without a doubt, what Billy Meier is seeing.

After shooting my last picture, the ship turned away over the tops of three firs and slowly withdrew northward into the sky where it stopped just beyond the trees. I took the last photo at 16:00, being the last frame on the roll of film. Only seconds after this last picture the stirring sound began again and the ship shot from a standing position by mad speed straight upwards into the cloudy sky and finally disappeared from view.

When Meier returned home from this first contact with this extra terrestrial woman, he sat down to write up what he could remember of the details of the experience and the conversation with the UFOnaut. When he began to write down the conversation, it came back to him word for word, just as it had been spoken, rapidly and clearly. This was his first experience with the new form of "transmission" that was soon perfected and refined to the extent that long and detailed dialogues were recaptured for the contact file.

First conversation with the UFOnaut:

UFO Woman	You are a fearless human being.
Meier	I have unlearned fear and have become objective.
UFO Woman	I know, because I have studied you for years.
Meier	Very nice, why is this?
UFO Woman	Because I want to make something clear to you.
Meier	Is nobody else suited for that?
UFO Woman	Surely, but we have provided you, because you have already occupied yourself for many years with this problem, and think really and sincerely like this as well.
Meier	Thanks for the flowers.
UFO Woman	No reason, because they are your own merit.
Meier	Well, but who are you really?
UFO Woman	Just call me "du" (you), as I do as well to you.
Meier	But who are you?
UFO Woman	I am called "Semjase," and I originate in the Pleiades.
Meier	In the Pleiades?
Semjase	Surely.
Meier	A nice walk, I would say. How did you perform such a walk—perhaps through hyper-space?
Semjase	You often know more than we desire.
Meier	Why so? I am closed (mouthed) and no chatterbox.
Semjase	I know, and because of that your knowledge is in the right place. I and others thus have no sorrows for that sake.
Meier	Why have you obstructed the way toward your ship against me? What about the film in my camera? Has it been destroyed?
Semjase	Certainly not, and you at least shall have photo proof.
Meier	I see. I ought to publicize, but how shall I arrange such?
Semjase	You will, and later I will explain the way for you.

Meier	Well then, but isn't this somewhat dangerous, to leave your ship landed so openly when other human beings may pass along here?
Semjase	Don't worry, because it is so provided that no other human being can come nearer than 500 meters in circumference around it. And besides this the beamship is protected by the forest and the hill against sight from very far.
Meier	Yes, then I am to become drawn into the meeting by myself alone.
Semjase	Yes, and you know why.
Meier	I understand, unfortunately.
Semjase	When you also regret it, there is nothing to change in this, nor in the future.
Meier	I also understand, my dear fellow creatures.
Semjase	Surely, their spiritual recognition has a long way to go. But you have taken the trouble and have learned. You have found the truth and have acquired knowledge. Because of this, you stand out from the great mass of human beings, and thus we have decided on you.
Meier	You always say "we." Does this mean, that....
Semjase	Surely, I have already said that you often know more than may be pleasant for us. Please keep silent about this, because the truth is already difficult enough for the human beings.
Meier	I have never owned this knowledge, and consequently I also cannot tell about it.
Semjase	You can also tell it, as you do, and I know that you will hush. I know that you would even contest all and the whole event, and offer it for fantasy if anyone should want to force you to speak.
Meier	You really know me very well.
Semjase	Thus we have chosen you, but enough of the questions and answers. Do listen now very thoroughly to what I have to tell you. Write everything down and go to the public with this then.
Meier	How can I, as I have nothing here for writing. I also have no recorder or anything similar.

Semjase	Don't worry about that, because you can write it down later. First, I will explain it all to you so that you have a survey. On the other hand, it is easier for me later to put myself in connection with you and give this into your thoughts, from which you can then write it all down word for word, everything very exactly.
Meier	Are you thinking of the same manner in which you brought me here?
Semjase	You really know too much, and make all honor for us.
Meier	Thank you.
Semjase	All right then. So do listen now and only interrupt me when you really do not understand.

Semjase's Explanation

Already for some time we have been urged to make contact with another Earth-human being, who really and sincerely wants to be helpful to our mission. Already very often we have tried this, but the human beings chosen were not knowledgeable enough or willing, and they also lacked sincerity and loyalty. And those we had selected for our endeavors feared for themselves and kept silence about our appearing. They insisted they would be abused and maybe harmed by officials and stupid-human intrigues, and be accused of lying. But despite that, many boastful humans come up, pretending contact with us and pretending they have even flown in the ships. Those are nothing more than deceivers who sun themselves in doubtful glory and want to profit from all. Earth humans have whole organizations which trouble themselves to explain our beamships, but above all there exists a few that really are authentic. They have many photos, which expose nothing more than some lights and light-appearances of natural origin, or quite conscious falsifications. Only very few of these photos are authentic and really show our beamships. Most of these photos are only creations of photographic deceit manufactured by cheaters and charlatans whose names become known worldwide by this. Their books and manuscripts written from this position are also a deception for the purpose of reputation and self-glory. On the other hand, many dare to connect us with the human religions, with which we want no concern in any way and any time. Your so-called sects don't shrink from this step, and themselves deceive their fellow creatures by such belief. These primitive machinations should stop before the whole world is overcome by such. If these deceivers were really in contact with us, and remained so, then we would have offered them a chance to get very clear photographic proof of our beamships. But as they are really not sincere humans, we have not given this chance to them. For evidence of this fact of truth, we gave you the chance to make distinct pictures of one of our beamships. Yet also further on, we will offer a chance for you to obtain still better and clearer picture evidence.

By the mid-1950s, a coterie of men claimed not only to have seen remarkable spacecrafts, but to have flown in them and to have talked at length with the occupants. They were known as contactees, and their stories so captured the public imagination that they completely thwarted Air Force efforts to downplay flying saucers. They also undermined the work of private UFO organizations searching seriously for answers.

The contactees, most notably George Adamski, Truman Bethurum, Orfeo Angelucci, Daniel Fry, and Howard Menger, each claimed to have been contacted by "space brothers" who gave them a "mission" to save the world from greed, corruption, and the atomic bomb. The space brothers took them aboard a Venusian, Saturian, Jupiterina, or Martian spaceship, where they saw beautiful women and received further instructions from Orthon, Aura, A-lan, and Neptune. They heard of idyllic conditions on their home planets, a situation to which the people of Earth could aspire. National interest was so great that over a hundred fifty flying saucer clubs sprang up dedicated just to them. In 1954 contactee George Van Tassel sponsored the first Giant Rock convention in Yucca Valley, California, a carnival affair with contactees giving lectures on their experiences and selling souvenirs from booths. Over five thousand people came.

After that, several of the contactees made outrageous claims. Howard Menger made the claim that he went to the moon, where he could breathe the air with little difficulty.

The Earth human beings called us extraterrestrials or star-people. He attributes to us supernatural acts and does not know us in the least. In truth we are human beings like the Earth human being, but our knowledge and wisdom are superior to his, as well as our technology. All right, the Earth human has taken his first very small step toward cosmic space flight, but this no more than the first primitive attempt. Even though he has reached the Moon by his missiles, he has not reached cosmic space. By this manner, he also would never reach it at any time, for necessary for this is an impulsion which is able to penetrate the hyperspace and dissolve the infinite distances. Space and time are not overcome by space and time, but by spacelessness and timelessness, which means that space and time collapse into one another and become equally directional to zero time. By that a few fractions of a second are enough to rush through billions of light-years, practically without loss of time, because zero-time neutralizes space and time simultaneously.

On other planets the forms of life are various—of human and animal sort. Also, many animal-like or even plant forms of life have developed to higher states. So there exists sorts that acquire much knowledge and free themselves from their life regions, and they also travel through the universe and here and there come to Earth.

Our major mission is aimed at your religions and the connected underdevelopment of the human spirit. Above everything there remains but one that possesses the power of life and death over each creature. This is the Creation alone, which has laid its laws over all. Laws that are irrefutable and of eternal validity. The human being can recognize them in nature when he troubles himself to do so. They expose for him the way of life and a way to spiritual greatness, embodying the goal of life. While the human indulges in his religions, and by this a heresy, he pines more and more away (in spirit), which finally leads to a bottomless abyss.

The human being may recognize that a god can never take over the part of the Creation or control the fate of a human being. A god is only a governor, and moreover a human being who exercises a powerful reign of tyranny over his fellow creatures. God is not the creation, but as well only a creature of it, like all dependent creatures. But the human being hunts for his religious wrong beliefs and affirms God being the Creation itself. He goes even further and pretends a normal earthman by the name of "Immanual," who is also called "Jesus Christ," is God's son and the Creation itself. Still different sects of the new age go on to maintain these same things, which already approach delusion.

Yet, as already mentioned, beamship deceivers also walk in the same direction and very clearly put out the lie to the world that we or our brothers and sisters from other planets of the cosmos would come at the order of God (with whom they mean the Creation) as angels or similar to bring the Earth human the long-hoped-for peace and the truth of religion and protection and order of God. That is nothing more than a well-considered falsehood from sectarians and deceivers. For we never had such orders, and we as well will never do that. The Creation itself gives the commands, because it embodies the greatest power in this Universe and never is in need of commands or religions. Religion is only the primitive work of human beings, in purpose to lead them, to suppress them, and for exploitation, to which only spiritually deficient life can fall.

Bring this truth to the light of the world and make it known. This is a further part of our mission. If this does not happen, then mankind will slowly destroy itself and fall into complete spiritual darkness.

We know that you (Meier) are aware of a secret old Scripture whose originals were unfortunately destroyed by the carelessness of our commissioner, who was your friend and who by regret has failed in fear. Diffuse and spread translation of this Scripture, because it is the only one that is authentic truth. And as we know, you also write about this scriptum and the truth. To us, it seems to be the most important book to be written, but it will be harsh in language and will meet with hate. It only offers the truth to Earth humans, though some speculations are in it. But it is finally able to destroy, for many, the madness of religion, or at least to temper it very deliberately. It is an extraordinary work, and you ought to make it accessible for human beings.

For the first time I have told you all that is necessary, but it cannot be enough. Many further contacts will follow after this first. And I will call you at a given point in time. But also by means of thought-transmission, which you call telepathy. I will get in contact with you and transmit further information. Do not worry that I will do this at a unsuitable time, but only then, when you want it. I know to regard your character and also your will for independence and thus I shall always direct myself to you.

The time will come for you when we will meet together in my beamship, and also when you will be allowed to undertake flight toward cosmic space with me. But for the next time such will not be possible; due to certain circumstances and regrettable occurrences this is not advisable. About this I will inform you at a later time in detail. So live well until the next time when I will give you further important information. But then the conversation should no more be so one-sided as today, when I had to explain to you. In the future each conversation will be quite normal, like is usual with questions and answers. See you again— and until soon...I say hello.

That was contact number one, 28 January 1975. After that the contacts went on, with anywhere from three to six per month until 16 September 1975, which was the thirty-fifth and last contact.

I am now going to pick out some of the more interesting things from various contacts. Some show advanced technical knowledge, some show advanced wisdom, and some show advanced religion, at least I think so.

The fourth contact: 15 February 1975. Advanced technology.

Meier: You speak a perfect German language. Where did you master this language?

Semjase: A good question that can be easily answered. Just like Earth humans, we have to learn a language. Yet this is much easier for us and less trouble. We possess all Earth languages, present and earlier, that were ever spoken. We have detailed knowledge of them in most different ways. From them language training courses are made, as you would call it. This work is performed by language-scientists and machines, similar to what you call computers. These machines serve, then, to transmit the desired language and instill it into us. This is performed in a machine-induced hypnotic-like state, and by this method the language terms and senses become implanted and registered. This process takes twenty-one days. Then we need another nine or ten days of practice to be able to speak the language correctly as well. This means we must train with the help of apparatus and language scientists as well for correct speaking and pronunciation. To learn one language takes about thirty to thirty-one days. In respect to this, Earth humans, especially at language institutes, are already using tape recorders in their language courses. This is already the first step in building apparatus and machines like ours and to put them into use. Such computers are already in research at different places of your Earth.

Advanced technology on space travel.

Semjase: For traveling through cosmic space, a drive is necessary that surpasses the speed of light by millions of times. But this propulsion can only come into action when the speed of light has already been reached. From that it follows that a further drive is needed to regulate normal speed up

	to the speed of light. This means that a beamship needs two drives—first the normal, which accelerates up to the speed of light, and then a second for hyperdrive, as you call it. A drive, then, that generates a million-fold and a billion-fold the speed of light, thus the hyper-speed by which hyper-space is penetrated. A space in which the mass increases in relation to speed. So time and space collapse, and they become zero time and zero space. This means time and space cease to exist. And exactly by that distances of numerous light-years are traversed in a fraction of a second, with no time lag.
Meier:	Does this mean that for a beamship and its passengers the same time passes as on the home planet?
Semjase:	Surely, when, for example, we leave the Pleiades and need about seven hours to get to Earth, then on our own planet, and on Earth, seven hours pass.

To me, this explanation of space-time is simpler and much easier to understand than any explanation we learned in Bob Lazar's science lesson.

Semjase didn't tell us Earth people how to produce the vast amount of power required to do space-time travel, thank God—or rather, thank Creation, because we are not evolved enough to be trusted with it. We would probably splatter ourselves and our planet all over our solar system!

However, because of this, I feel entirely justified in revealing the secrets of the U.S. government in Area S4, where they are attempting to back-engineer several alien spaceships.

Whoever on Earth is successful at producing a spaceship with anti-matter as fuel also has an energy force capable of destroying the Earth. Here again, as Semjase stated, our only hope would be a complete union of all nations on Earth.

Meier:	How is it possible for a beamship in the gravity of a planet, or in its atmosphere, to attain such great speeds without glowing or the passengers succumbing to the huge pressures?
Semjase:	This is very easy to explain. The beamship is surrounded by a protection beam screen, which allows every interference to glide away without pushing. The same also hap-

pens in the cosmos, which swarms with particles. So the beam protection screen functions to protect the ship against all influences and resistances, with anything contacting the screen disintegrating or "flowing" away. All penetrating or resistance-offering things are simply diverted without evoking pressure. A pressure would mean resistance and would inhibit unlimited speed. But removal of the protective screen initiates another important effect that is of great importance to the passenger. The glide-away effect of the beam protection screen also neutralizes the attractive force of a planet—which results in the beamship not being subject to the gravitational forces of the planet. The gravity of a planet is, besides this, not always the same, or of the same strength, owing to certain alternations that will be discovered by your scientists in a reasonable time. The beam protective screen diverts the gravity and attractive forces, and the beamship in effect becomes a miniature planet that can travel at nearly lightspeed through any atmosphere without risk. As the gravity of a concerned planet does not influence the beamship, the passengers feel normal and unburdened. They feel as if they are on their own planet, always under the premise that the planetary gravity is in accordance with their anatomical capabilities. In the beamship itself, the gravity is tuned to the passengers and is completely controllable. When passengers on spacecraft from other worlds move in atmospheres alien to them, or on hostile planets with unbearable gravity, they use suits and small transportable instruments that generate for that creature the necessary beam protective screen for its particular requirement.

Many hundreds or even thousands of people have seen UFOs suddenly shoot straight up, and in an instant be out of sight. Or they have seen them traveling at thousands of miles per hour, and then make a right-angle turn. Travis Walton, after he was returned to Earth, witnessed the spaceship that had delivered him suddenly shoot straight up and instantly out of sight. He wondered how, like all of the rest of them, this was possible without the ship burning up like the space shuttle or the occupants killed by G forces.

This explanation by Semjase is so straightforward and explains it so well that, to me, it leaves no doubt that their scientific knowledge far surpasses ours on Earth.

The Eighteenth Contact, Thursday, 15 May 1975
Semjase: Before today we were discussing other things, but today I want to continue with the discussion of spirit. A person may react to the word or the designation "the Creation" in different ways, as though it were something apart and beautiful and good. Such is not exactly the case. Such characterizations as "omnipresent," "all powerful," and "all knowing" are valid characterizations of the nature of the Creation. Millions of religious humans do not understand the true nature of the Creation. Whenever they speak of it, they tend to personify it as a God-being (which is then itself a separation from the Creation), and they confuse the idea of the Creation. So it is very important to know as much as possible about the character and the nature of the Creation, for when the word is understood properly it buoys the inner mind and connects it to its source as soon as the word is heard.

The experience reveals the Creation as unlimited beauty, harmony, knowledge, and truth...enduring endlessly. So whenever a human perceives a thing of beauty—a flower, an animal, clouds, water, landscape, music, color, etc.—he considers it in connection with the limitless grandeur of the Creation itself. When a human recognizes and realizes this, then he knows that this recognition springs from limitness cognition; even inside the tiniest creature, like a microbe, he sees the limitless Creation.

The Creation is inside of every human being (and every other Creation and thing), being a fraction of that manifestation itself. Once this thought has penetrated deeply inside a person and he can experience it, he loses all fear and doubt. When he knows his contact is with knowing, almighty Creation he will enjoy peace and tranquility. Reflection on this gives the name "Creation" great meaning. The more he meditates on this reality, the more his intelligence is illuminated and the more powerful his personality becomes. His whole life and labor is blessed. The Creation rises in his consciousness and he senses peace, strength, knowledge, and wisdom, delight, and hope. He can overcome obstacles and achieve his objectives, and he suddenly has no more need for purely material things. One must learn a spiritual-intellectual manner of thinking and recognize its validity until the first successes are achieved.

By the way, it does not stop here. Further exploration, research, development, and recognition lead to limitless endurance of time. Everything may happen in the course of time to prevent one from achieving his objectives, but the spiritualized person knows no limit and does not allow himself to be stopped short of his goals of any events of the future. For him the future always exists in the present, where he becomes determined to do everything here and now to obtain the highest spiritual state of consciousness. He does not fear the future for the future is now—just as present as the present itself.

When the spiritualized being sees others before him, he sees the Creation in them.

The Thirty-first Contact, Thursday, 17 July 1975
The Ride on the Great Spacer
Edward Meier made plans for an absence of thirty hours and prepared himself for this anticipated trip. He got up early, carefully bathed and dressed, loaded his bike, and started out for the remote and very secluded rendezvous spot selected by the female cosmonaut.

Arriving at the signified location, he unloaded his equipment and hid his bike against accidental discovery. Shortly after this the spacecraft arrived and was greeted by the extraterrestrial woman Semjase.

Semjase:	Today is your big day.
Meier:	After all you have told me, I feel the same way.
Semjase:	You had to think about what would be expected. But now I must explain at this time what you have to keep silent about certain concerns. At a later time I will be able to allow you to tell about the experience. From that I will leave out of the transmission of the report certain things of which you may not speak. But come now; first we make a journey through your solar system.

We go to the ship and are lifted inside by the transport beam. Only a few seconds after this the ship floats up high, and from about 50 meters up I shoot up some dia-pictures of the environment of the departure point. I can take these pictures through the entrance hatch as we climb very slowly higher. After shooting the pictures, Semjase closes the hatch, and within seconds the ship rushes up to several kilometers in height without my noticing any pressure or any other change. Everything is just like I was standing on solid ground on the Earth. Different alternations of the course produce no bodily effect, though I can see through the "windows" on board that at different times we shoot along in the craziest movements, like a great pendulum.

Semjase:	We will now leave the gravity field of Earth.
Meier:	To where shall we go now?
Semjase:	At first to Venus, where you may first use your camera.
Meier:	What about Venusians? Can we photograph them?
Semjase:	You like to joke...
Meier:	I only wanted to see what you would say.
Semjase:	Your ways of thinking can often be troublesome. But look here now: We have produced this apparatus here to give you better possibilities for getting better photographs. You can hold your camera against this screen and then photograph outside. As you see, you are able to look through this transparent material to outside, as if it were a simple pane of glass. In that way you can obtain better color pictures...we hope. For our part, we have another. And now you suddenly come up with a suitable camera.
Semjase:	[Laughing quietly] This camera is a product of your technology, which one of us obtained.
Meier:	This surprises me, as then you would have to go into our villages or towns.
Semjase:	Is that so strange for you?
Meier:	I see only [space] dresses and with these, neither you nor any others of you could walk [undiscovered] before the eyes of the Earth humans.
Semjase:	Surely, but we also own dresses of your fashion. We do need these, because here and there we walk in your circles.
Meier:	That actually does not surprise me, but why don't you go out for an evening with me?
Semjase:	About this matter, we make a date.
Meier:	That is nice, but with us we have the so-called police,

who sometimes check on different persons. What will
happen if somebody demands from you your personal
[identification] papers?

Semjase: Don't worry about this. If that should happen, then we
are able to take care of this by thought-influencing. We
produce by the force of our thinking, sham-pictures for
the concerned questioners. The police officers, or others,
would then in fact be of the opinion that they really had
in their hands the passport, etc., and would examine
these.

Meier: But that's cheating, Semjase.

Semjase: No, it deals only with the question of hallucination, if you
want to term it this way.

Meier: I understand, but we better leave from this theme.

Semjase: Now you can get some pictures of Venus's stratum. Then
I will show you the surface of the planet itself. By regret I
can only do this via the viewing screen and the "window."
The special viewing screen of the device for photographing will have to be closed because of the high temperatures of this planet. The screen is more able to resist cold,
but not such great heat. But do not be disappointed
about the appearance of this world. The planet is in a
stage of first development of primitive life.

Meier: You have already mentioned this, so I am not disappointed.

Semjase: Surely, but still there are different things here about
which you have to keep silent.

[I quickly shoot the allowed pictures; then the beamship drives away
from its position and rushes toward Venus. Immensely dense masses of
clouds suddenly surround us, and of the most different coloration. This
cover of clouds is unbelievably many kilometers deep, and there seems to be
no end as we are sinking down through it to reach the surface of the planet. But finally we have penetrated so far, and the clouds change density and
open up. There at nearly 40 kilometers in height we leave the last cloud formations, and I see the surface of Venus on two different viewing screens.
The landscape is wild looking and crater covered. Only in parts may be seen
not-too-high mountains. At one side I see a huge mountainless area that is

full of craters. Semjase now points out a polar region, she says, and the mountains do not extend this far.]

Meier:	But that's nearly all empty and lifeless, Semjase. It looks to me like a second moon.
Semjase:	Surely, this I have explained to you.
Meier:	But what is that down there—there beside the crater?
Semjase:	An exploration sonde from your Earth.
Meier:	I see. What is it like? If you would curve around the planet two or three times, so that I can see as well other regions and the night side, would...
Semjase:	Surely I also intend to do this.
Meier:	Thank you.

[And already Semjase speeds the ship around Venus. Certain observational discoveries are not allowed to be explained at this time.]

Semjase:	The next aim is to Mercury, and then we go to the greater planets, which you have already seen one time. But certain matters which you will see you are not allowed to tell others.
Meier:	That's all right. You know I will behave according to your wishes.

We fly toward different planets of this solar system, where several times I take pictures, but only at greater distance. Close-up photos or pictures of details are not allowed by Semjase. She gives no further information for this behavior. During the whole time, different very important matters were discussed, about which, unfortunately, only so much is allowed to be explained. Some of their existing forms of life are completely different in character than humans, and as well are not interested in Earth human beings. As an exception, there are different existing surface stations of extraterrestrial intelligence, other forms of life that are not at home on the sole planets but are just stationed there for certain missions. When we are again back over Earth, I see in space different space objects besides the two satellites (Apollo and Soyus), and I can see five other objects, which are surely space crafts of extraterrestrial origin. In response to a question on this, Semjase affirms that only one of the five belongs to them while the other four ships are of other races visiting our planets who are here to observe the linking of the "Apollo-Soyus" capsules. Peculiarly, I cannot see those objects through the "windows," but only on the screen of the beamship. Semjase explains that all the extraterrestrial ships are masked from sight and can only be seen on their zero-sight picture screens. The zero-sight screen is explained as including a special viewing means that is able to pick up all that the eye and less sophisticated methods like radar beams cannot see. I am satisfied by this explanation as Semjase does not want to go into detail.

It stands to reason that the four extraterrestrial space ships would have themselves masked from view. Being from outer space, they would all have space distortion drives, and this ability to make themselves invisible is a form of space distortion. So the "Apollo" and the "Soyus" astronauts had many observers watching the linkup.

Then I turned my attention to a newly appearing object, high over the Earth on the horizon, invisible to all human eyes, and outside of all possibilities of viewing with Earth technical apparatus. We quickly approach the new object and fly only a short distance from it. It is the "Soyus" space capsule, which will be linked with the "Apollo" capsule. Clearly I can see the letters "CCCP" painted there in large letters. I know this capsule contains two living Russian humans and, peculiarly touched, I turn for that reason to Semjase.

Meier:	To me this whole undertaking is crazy. Inside of this small gondola are two living human beings.
Semjase:	It is true. The capsules are very small and offer really no space for living. I know, you fear to think that you might be there inside. You have good reason to feel like that.
Meier:	You speak in riddles, Semjase.
Semjase:	In time you will understand my words, but do you want to see inside the capsule?
Meier:	How will this be possible? The object is closed and sealed all around.
Semjase:	You do not know the possibilities of our technology, which allows us to distort any matter in such a way by our radiations so that it becomes invisible to the eye. We are able to do this in a very strictly controlled manner and can guide the effect very exactly in this respect.

Meier: Then please let me see your wonder-piece.

[Semjase occupies herself with some apparatus, while I very interestedly look through the specially built viewing screen for photographs, in the direction of the Soyus capsule. Very suddenly a part of the capsule quite simply disappears, and I look in astonishment on the two human beings who rest lying within the seats, which look like loafers or something like that. Without intending, I spoke to Semjase because of that.]

Meier: Semjase, there....
Semjase: Do not fear, because nothing happens to them. To them the matter of the capsule is still the same as before, because only for us it has become transparent to sight.
Meier: But that is nothing more than a flying metal coffin, Semjase! The men are really squeezed into this box. And how is anybody able to shoot this thing up here, because everything is really so primitive? Just look at that inside equipment and apparatus—really primitive.
Semjase: Be not excited; they will get back to Earth again, quite well. Everything may look quite primitive, by which you express the right word, but consider here that you Earth beings are just at the beignning of space-exploration, so to speak, still standing in the baby shoes. Because of that your technologies cannot yet be very highly developed.
Meier: That may be correct, but when I look at your ship, then....
Semjase: Here you cannot make any comparisons, as our technologies are thousands of years in advance of yours. From your level this primitive capsule and its equipment represents a very imnportant and highly developed technology. So you should not be so unjust, as the differences between you and us are too much.
Meier: Yes, that's all right—but this flying metal coffin...
Semjase: Don't worry about it, but look there now. That is the second capsule, and inside it are three humans.
Meier: Oh, yes, the Americans. At what time will the miracle occur?
Semjase :   In a few minutes the final maneuvering will start. Do start now shooting pictures, in which I will assist you.

After linking the two capsules, which will happen soon, you can photograph some different satellites of Earth and of extraterrestrial origin too. After that we will depart for our great-spacer one station in this system, with which we will then go to different systems....where I have to fulfill a mission. There also should be a surprise for you too, but now pay attention to your task.

(I attentively watch the two space-capsules drift slowly toward each other. I notice that the "Apollo" capsule of the Americans is decisively greater than the "Soyus." Semjase explains it this way. The "Apollo" capsule of the Americans is larger because it is carrying the linking apparatus, which will serve as the transfer-channel from one capsule to the other. This linking mechanism, after finishing its task, will be released from the "Apollo" and be allowed to "just drift away." I work with my camera and together with Semjase, who is now beside me with a second camera. Semjase works her apparatus, and this time I can see both capsules and the connecting link, and of course again all the humans inside. In the "Apollo" I notice that the space is much greater than the "Soyus," and the capsule of the Americans is decisively more richly instrumental. I now have to laugh, as I observe one of the Americans floating without gravity) bump his head on something. And he touches his hand to his skull. I do not know which man because I know none of these capsule-dwellers by name or by picture. Now Semjase switches off her instruments and the linked capsules are normal again.)

Semjase: The time has come to move for the meeting with the great-spacer.

(Without further word, she starts the beamship moving again, and already a few minutes later the Earth has shrunk to a great star, which shines bluely through space. Having seen this before, I turn to Semjase, who sits in her peculiarly shaped chair, guiding the beamship through the dark space in which are billions of stars clearer and more distinct than they can be seen from Earth. It is truly fantastic picture that I will never forget. Among the great and small stars are groups and clusters and the big band of the Milky Way, immeasurable in size and beauty. At that time Semjase disturbs me in my considerations and thoughts.)

| Semjase: | Now look to the front. There is our great-spacer, which will take us aboard. |

(At a difficult-to-estimate distance hangs a huge metal sphere in the dark space, reflecting only weakly the light of the sun. Very slowly now the speed of the beamship decreases. Semjase is sitting very attentively before her apparatus and instruments and steers wisely and carefully in the direction of the huge sphere, which looks to me like a small planet. Several luminous lens-shaped ships were moving in the vicinity in a formation. One left the formation and performed a strange somersaulting maneuver, which I photographed. I can see, way down in the lower third, a little to the left, that a yawning port is open. I recognize this as an entrance hatch, no doubt a hangar into which we are now slowly flying. Innumerable beamships of the same type as ours are standing there in orderly rows, and only 100 by 100 meters square of the hangar entrance is cleared. I look back at the hangar entrance and can see that the wall is shifting itself and closes the hatch. Everything all around is brightly illuminated, and the light, which appears a bit blue, seems to come from directly out of the walls. The whole hangar is very huge and according to these sizes this spherical ship has to be gigantic.)

| Meier: | How big is this spaceship, Semjase? |
| Semjase: | It is very large, very very large even, and it is the greatest of its sort. It is a very special ship that embodies all technologies known to us. Altogether it is its own perfect world, a world which is able to fly almost anywhere. It hides inside a complete inhabited city of 144,000 resident. Everything needed for living can be produced inside the ship itself, and it is absolutely independent of anything of any kind from outside its cover. This spaceship represents our newest development and is working together with different other ones of its kind. They are finding useful applications for intersteller missions and for keeping order. They are able to move within all systems and all spaces, and also for them negotiating the barrier between universes is no more any obstacle. We are just at the first of these great missions. |

Meier:	Fantastic. If I understand you right, as you explained, then you are able, with this great ship, like others of its class....
Semjase:	You have understood me right.
Meier:	Then do tell me one thing, please. You have formally told me that you knew Asket well?
Semjase:	Surely.
Meier:	Where did you know Asket, and what do you know about her and her race? And what do you know in this connection about her and I?
Semjase:	There is no secret. Asket has explained all to me, and from that I know that about ten years ago you were together in contact. All details are known to me, as well as your time-travels into the past with her help.
Meier:	You are frighteningly open, Semjase. Asket has forbidden me to speak of this; before she would permit me to do so by a sign.
Semjase:	You have just received the sign.
Meier:	You mean that you're just now indicating knowledge that this is the sign?
Semjase:	Yes, surely, but you are still obliged to limit speaking in this respect. You still must maintain silence about the time-travel and what you have learned. You are now allowed to publish your written reports about your contact with Asket in 1964. Have you preserved them well?
Meier:	Of course. I have just waited for the permission to speak, and have preserved it all well. But how does it happen actually, that you know Asket?
Semjase:	After the break-off of her contact with you in 1964 in India, she contacted our high council and succeeded in obtaining their cooperation. With the help of her race, from the "Dal-Universe," we obtained knowledge of higher technical capabilities and received the most exact data that assisted us in further development of these great spaceships. That data now is being put to good use. Here, we can now leave our ship because the room is atmospherically balanced and prepared.

(By the transport beam we let ourselves slide out of the hatch and stand on the metal floor of the great-spacer. For the first time now, as I am outside the beamship, I realize that the cleared landing space is surrounded by clear glass walls, and the innumerable other beamships are beyond these walls. Between these parked ships many human beings are rushing along who quite evidently occupy themselves with the various ships. But I also see walking, mechanical apparatuses quite like some kind of robots, who as well are hurrying all around and executing various works. Very far beyond, I am just able to see some bigger beamships, which are of a form completely different from the ones hitherto known to me. Semjase occupies herself with a small thing in her hand. Before us the transparent wall opens and reveals an entrance. Then I notice a completely silent small vehicle floating near, not much bigger than a Volkswagon car. It floats close to 20 cm above the floor surface, and it is equipped with very comfortable seats inside. Semjase calls me to take one of the seats beside her, and the strange-moving vehicle floats away and rises slowly higher and higher. I look back and see that the transparent wall closes itself again, after our ship was brought by the already seen robots into the main hangar-hall. The hangar-hall seems to take up this whole lower part of the space giant. The ceiling above, like the walls, radiates a soft blue light. It looks like a sky, and if I am not mistaken, there exactly in the center is a great hole. Soon I can see this is so, as there is an opening in the direction we are now floating in our transportation vehicle, and we climb up inside this opening. Also inside this shaft is a gentle blue illumination, which comes from the walls. For minutes we climb up with increasing speed, until Semjase suddenly moves the floating vehicle into to a side wall and stops. Here is another area about 100 by 100 meters, and I feel myself suddenly thrust into a world of marvels. Wherever I look I see green fields, trees, bushes, and flowers. This is a real little "Garden of Eden" in this space giant.)

Meier:	This is fantastic, Semjase.
Semjase:	It is almost natural, as I told you, because this spaceship is its own independent small world.
Meier:	You speak easily, but I am seeing this for the first time. I am completely overwhelmed. But how high are we in here in fact?
Semjase:	I don't understand what you mean?

Meier:	I mean, how far have we floated up until now, inside of this giant. How many meters?
Semjase:	About to 11,000 meters. We have stopped here near the center of the ship, where exists the actual town of 144,000 people.

I have calculated the area of this place where 144,000 people live using 11,000 meters as the radius, and it comes out to 146 square miles. This is equal to a 12 mile by 12 mile piece of ground. It seems reasonable that 144,000 people could live there.

Meier:	Dear me. Oh, then during this short time we have climbed up by means of this vehicle, higher than our highest mountain on Earth, Mount Everest.
Semjase:	We have climbed up very quickly; in that you are right. But concerning Mount Everest, I have to correct you, as it is not the highest mountain on Earth.
Meier:	Now you make me laugh, Semjase. Mount Everest is indeed the highest mountain on my dear mother Earth.
Semjase:	My words are true—they are a matter of fact. But of course you can't know this, as you start from the reason-based premise. Your scientists count the height of a country or of a mountain in "meters above sea level." There exactly is the mistake, for such measurements should not use sea-level as the starting point. The starting point for all measurements should be from the center of the planet, which never changes. This is because planets are never exactly round, but tend more toward an elliptical shape. But in truth, Mount Everest is 2150 meters shorter than the highest mountain of your world. When you measure Earth mountains, then the center of the planet is decisive, and measured from there, you will see, the highest mountain is not Mount Everest.
Meier:	I understand. Your explanation is very illuminating. The earth has become elliptical by the Earth's rotation, and as far as I know the Andes of South America is where we should find the highest mountains.

Semjase:	We walk now through the park's facilities to another transport pit, which will lift up to the control center. It is located at the top in a cupola of this great spacer craft. There the leader of this ship is waiting.
Meier:	I shall enjoy it, Semjase. What rank has this leader?
Semjase:	In your terms, one could say "governor" likely, or even "king."
Meier:	I see, and to speak to the utmost chief of this giant ship, don't wait for a genuflection by me when I stand in front of him. Such jokes are not my line. Even before the dear God in person, I would not chafe my knees.
Semjase:	The leader is a "IHWH."
Meier:	That is all the same to me, and if he wants me to polish the ground in front of him, then he ought to do this in front of me first.
Semjase:	I see you really feel this way.
Meier:	Do you think I would joke about that? I regard a human being as simply a human being, whether he is from this world or another.
Semjase:	(Suddenly laughing. Then more laughing behind in the park, and suddenly the other sounds like male laughter, which ends abruptly.) You are good; you are really good.
Meier:	What does that mean, and what about this laughter down from the ceiling, which has stopped so quickly?
Semjase:	(Laughing) He had...he has turned off the speaker system, and he is surely laughing up there in the cupola.
Meier:	You mean, that has been the dear god of the box? Has he eavesdropped on us?
Semjase:	Surely...this has been...but please don't call him "Dear God," because this evokes painful memories about our very early development. We have already maintained this application of "IHWH," but it now has for us a completely new meaning.
Meier:	If that's the way it is....
Semjase:	Thank you. It has been a funny joke.
Meier:	I only hold my opinion, and I don't think it funny, because I meant it earnestly.

Semjase: Surely, and we shall honor your thoughts, but to us it has
             been a joke. You were so serious and used expressions
             which revealed your feelings clearly. Now let's go.

(We slowly walk a little ways through the park. The paths are soft and
not of metal, they are made of some artificial soil or similar matter. Here is
a fantastic world of flowers, of often completely strange blossoms and scents.
But I also see flowers and bushes and trees exactly like I know on Earth. We
need only a few minutes to cross the park. Then we stand again before a
transportation pit, with a vehicle floating gently in it, which we now use for
further driving, if I may use this term. With increasing speed we float higher again, and suddenly there is a free sky above us. As far as my eyes can see
and reach, I am viewing the infinite vastness of the universe. Stars shine,
and I ask myself how we could simply float out there, because we should not
be able to live up here where there is no air. Then we reach the end of the
shaft where there is the cupola about which Semjase had spoken. A giant
area exists here of desk-like formations into which apparatus and screens
have been installed. Before them are human beings and a form of life
unknown to me that I soon recognize as being mechanical—real human
machines, androids. This complete cockpit is a giant cupola of several kilometers in diameter. Over and above is seen the free cosmos, and I wonder
that I can breathe. Then I remember the completely transparent walls of
the hangar, and it becomes evident to me that the whole cupola consists of
this transparent material. So I ask Semjase about it.)

Meier: Semjase, can you explain to me what kind of matter is
             this transparent material which is forming this cupola? Is
             it a kind of glass?
Semjase: No, that is not glass. It is a very stable metal alloy, as also
             are the walls of the beamship.
Meier: Dear....
Semjase: Remember the Earth space-capsules into which you were
             able to look?
Meier: You meanthat everything is made transparent by apparatus?
Semjase: Surely, all walls as well as the cupola of the most hard
             metal. But the radiation generated by our apparatus can
             make them appear transparent. To the eye then, it looks
             like nothing is there.

Meier:	Fantastic.
Semjase:	Come now.

(And we float on in the vehicle toward the middle of the huge command center. I see there a horseshoe shaped formation about one meter high. It is completely covered with apparatus and picture screens, and altogether it is not much bigger than the average room. A single human being is standing inside this horseshoe formation and looks toward us. When Semjase brings our transportation vehicle to land on a marked area about 60 meters from the horseshoe, the waiting human being comes toward us. I now see clearly that he is wearing a dress similar to that of Semjase, and there is a look of love and friendliness on his face. I estimate him to be about seventy or seventy-five years old. Now Semjase gets out of the vehicle and hurries toward the old man, who also moves quickly to Semjase. Then they are together and embrace one another. This I consider really human-like and not much different from our own earthly form of greeting. Anyhow, a pain touches me that I am not able to define. But I push away the feeling and walk slowly toward both, who are now speaking to each other. Yet I cannot understand a single word because the language is completely strange to me. But then I come up to them and see the older man who is watching me smile knavishly. Then Semjase speaks to me.)

Semjase: This is my father.

(At first I am astonished. Then I push my hand out, which is seized by the man and pressed. It is a gentle but firm pressure, like that of Semjase. I confess to being confused, or just beaten, because I would never have expected to see Semjase's father. Then the pleasant voice of the man sounds to me.)

Semjase's father:It is a great delight for me, seeing you here. Semjase has already reported very much to me about you. Be welcomed here with us.

(Again I wonder; the father of Semjase is speaking the same good German as Semjase herself does.)

Meier: Thank you very much.

(I cannot say more because now Semjase's father encloses me into his arms and welcomes me. Quite suddenly I am unable to speak as a confounded lump is in my throat. The devil may know why. Semjase seems to sense this, for she speaks once more to her father in that incomprehensible language. He then turns to me.)

Semjase's father:Call me "Ptaah." Possibly it has meaning for you, as in former times it was used on Earth.

Meier: What?

Ptaah: I see you do not know the connection. An ancestor has been, in former times, on your Earth and lived as one of your people. He was an "IHWH" and was related by matrimony to his wife "BASTH." He used the same name as I, Ptaah. On your Earth you still have very old traditions, tales, and legends about him.

Meier: By regret that is not known to me, but I will search in this respect in our books to see if I can find something.

Semjase: You surely will, if you trouble yourself about South American stories of gods. Therein lie many beginnings. In most cases they are connected to events concerning Venus and other planets of your solar system.

Part Two of this book is titled "The Proof of Ancient Astronaughts, Alias Anunnaki, Alias Nefiln." It is based on Zecharia Sitchin's interpretation of the ancient clay tablet, mostly from Mesopotamia. As you will see when you read Part Two, it is very well researched, and I believe quite accurate.

Semjase's father's name is Ptaah and he had an ancestor by the same name, who was involved in ancient South American stories of gods.

Enki's Egyptian name was Ptah [Sitchin spelled it with one a]. He shared the African continent with his sons; among them was the firstborn MAR.DUK whom the Egyptians called Ra, NIN.GISH.ZI.DA whom the Egyptians called Thoth.

On page 84 in Zecharia Sitchin's book *The Lost Realms* he stated the following.

It is my belief that it was the same Thoth, alias Quetzalcoatl, who had bestowed the calendar of Fifty-Two, and all other knowledge, upon the people of Mesoamerica. In the Yucatan the Maya called him Kukulcan; in the Pacific regions of Guatemala and in El Salvador he was called Xiuhtecuhtli. The names all meant the same: Feathered or Winged Serpent.

At first temples were lofted atop step Pyramids to worship the Serpent God, and the skies were observed to watch for key celestial cycles. But there came a time when the God—or all the celestial gods—had left. Seen no more.

But had not Quetzalcoatl promised to return?

Fervently the skywatchers of the jungles consulted ancient almanacs. Priests advanced the notion that the vanished deities would return if offered the throbbing heart of human victims.

But at some crucial calendrical date in the ninth century A.D., a prophesied event failed to occur. All the cycles came together and added to naught. And so the ceremonial centers and cities dedicated to the gods were abandoned, and the jungle cast its green mantle over the domain of the serpent god.

Ptaah: Come now, we are already on the move to our "transmit" position.

[In fact, I see that outside the cupola the star position are slowly changing. We must be driving at great speed. But I have noticed nothing about the gigantic spaceship starting to move. Now we are all three sitting in very comfortable chairs at the horseshoe-shaped console. On picture screens are the bodies of our sun system and many other great and small stars and other things to see. I nearly lose my eyes—so much different and fantastic it all is.... We must be moving fast. I ask Ptaah about it.]

Meier: Ptaah, how fast are we flying now?
Ptaah: Look here, this instrument shows the velocity. You can read it very easily yourself, even if you do not understand our symbols or units of measure. In your understanding, these lines are like decimals, and these sharp arrow-headed branches show this hundreds nominators. These haft-crossing lines mark the thousands, and these points line the hundred-thousands. These ring lines here mean for you something like the speed of light. Now you can just read together the values and by that combine the speed yourself.

Meier:	Yes...a moment... [I count very carefully, and I reach a result of 89 values in the decimal field, and then two point lines and eleven values.] That's fantastic! [Now, after seeing all this advanced, unbelievable technology, I ask the question.] How long will it take until we are as far on Earth?
Ptaah:	Perhaps another thousand years in your chronology.
Meier:	Here I am curious. How long will we fly through the cosmos—like we are now?
Ptaah:	Still about thirty minutes, then we will "transmit" to another system.
Meier:	Transmit? That's "time traveling" isn't it?
Semjase:	Surely, but such is already known to you.
Meier:	Do we still have time before we transmit?
Semjase:	Certainly.
Meier:	Well, you spoke down there in the park about our dear IHWH, who had eavesdropped on us by the speaker installation. When can I see him and where? Is he perhaps troubling himself to come here?

[Semjase and Ptaah start laughing again, then Semjase speaks.]

Semjase:	You have already saluted him.
Meier:	[Some seconds pass before I understand.] Oh, that— dear, dear. The father of Semjase, Ptaah, is the leader of this space giant, an "IHWH," a good God himself, in person! Oh, that just slipped off my tongue. I really did not want to...
Ptaah:	Please don't worry about it. I already understand. We have come to our point of transmission.

[Ptaah and Semjase turn themselves to the instruments at the horseshoe-shaped formation. Small light-bodies shine up, and a dark picture screen comes alive. For the first time I hear a tone, a very soft and calming singing of metal. I look up at the transparent cupola and see the scene suddenly wash away in a whitish milky veil. This only lasts a very short moment, and already I can see stars moving. But that also is for only a few seconds; then they shift along slowly as before. At the whole realization I feel somehow peculiar, but I feel a great tranquility inside myself. Then I hear the voice of Semjase. I wonder about this as Ptaah had asked for silence: did something have to be delayed with the transmission?]

Meier:	But what is the matter? Is there no success with the transmission?
Semjase:	Why haven't you noticed?
Meier:	I have, but I can't explain it...
Semjase:	Then you need only to look out the cupola into space. Now, what do you see there?

[I follow instructions, and I am astonished.]

Meier:	Girl, there are completely other formations than those I know from Earth. Why is that?
Semjase:	You are around 500 light-years from our home-world. There—look there. Above that formation of stars there, that is our home world; these are the Pleiades. We are only 211 million kilometers from the nearest star. Unfortunately we cannot arrive closer because we need a safe distance to be able to transmit again. Perhaps you can succeed in getting some pictures with the apparatus, which has been brought from the beamship.

[Coming from somewhere, an android appears, bringing the photographic device. Very cleverly it assembles it and places it in order. Suddenly the thing speaks to me, and once more I am flattered, although I understand not a word. Semjase quickly enlightens me.]

Semjase:	It wishes you good success.
Meier:	But that's impossible. Can this thing think and act independently? That would be crazy.
Ptaah:	But nevertheless it does.
Semjase:	Its whole bodily construction is half-organic, and its brain is chemical.
Ptaah:	It is highly developed. You will understand this after a short time, when it is more normal for you. It is only the

newness that makes it strange. But take care now about the pictures because the next leap is being prepared...

Ptaah: Watch the stars...In nine seconds we start the next jump.

[I do as advised and experience it all again like the first time. But this time the process is much more familiar. Now I understand the peculiarity. During the split second I feel once more a deep tranquility, now more familiar to me than the first time.]

Meier: Oh my....

Ptaah: We have reached our next stop. The nebulous formation you see far in front is what you call the "Orion Nebula." It is about 1,800 light-years from here to your Earth.

Meier: Can I get some pictures?

Semjase: Surely, if they succeed for you.

[Again I trouble myself with shooting pictures. If they come out only fair, then I am satisfied. Lost in thought, I work automatically. My own thoughts remain on the eternity. The feeling was so great and powerful that all words fail me. At the next leap I want to observe myself. I want to see whether I become nebulous like the milky mass and whether I feel anything inside me. It...)

Ptaah: [Reading my thoughts, interrupts] This will be possible, if you watch very carefully for it. [After a few seconds we start the next leap. I realize his words only halfway, because my thoughts were elsewhere. I concentrate my eyes on myself and wonder. Then quite suddenly I cannot see my body, and in another split second it is normal. The first thing I notice is my watch and I remember that whenever I came too near Semjase's beamship, my watch always went too fast or too slow. It strangely seems to be running normally now.

Later, Billy Meier asks Semjase, "Would it be possible sometime to give me some written lines from you?"

Semjase was very hesitant. She said, "Is that so important? And how shall I do this, as I don't have the necessary utensils, and I do not master your script. We ourselves use completely different symbols for writing."

After much discussion about what she should write, Semjase said "Please let's not speak of this anymore. Come give me the paper and the writer."

Billy Meier gives her the paper and the felt writer without a word, and she now starts writing without hesitation. She finishes her writing.

Meier: You have written this all very kindly, and I myself am delighted with it. Now I have a question about this script: How old is this writing, and where does it originate?

Semjase: That's easy to explain: These letters we are using are only 11,000 years old, and we had taken them over at that time from our ancestors who lived on Earth. Our older letters and script form was much more complex, while this is much easier. This script form was developed by our scientists on Earth, who used for a pattern the seen from Earth star formations. They connected certain star pictures by lines; the circles represent stars and the lines just connect them.

Meier: That's interesting, and your explanation suffices for me in that this script is no more known on Earth.

Semjase: It has only been forgotten, but was in used many centuries ago, during which it was often changed in detail. Still some scripts of Earth humans are simply altered forms of these shapes that have been made into letters, which trace back to our old symbols.

Meier: This is astonishing! Then the script on Earth was not developed by Earth men themselves?

Semjase: If you speak of earthbound forefathers of your human races, and not of the heavenly ancestors, then you are correct. It was first brought by the "Sons of Heaven," who were responsible for the reemergence of Earth humans from savagery.

[As you will see later, Zecharia Sitchin in his writing about ancient astronauts, called them "Anunnaki," which meant "those who from Heaven to Earth came." This is exactly what Zecharia Sitchin says, which is that *Homo sapiens* were created by genetic manipulation of the Anunnaki (Sons of Heaven) and Homo erectus (Savagery).]

See Figure 4, in which Sitchin shows how ancient scripts are altered forms of many of the letters in our alphabet. Figure 5 was taken out of a Webster dictionary and shows the similarity between Hebrew, Arabic, Greek, Russian, and Sanskrit.

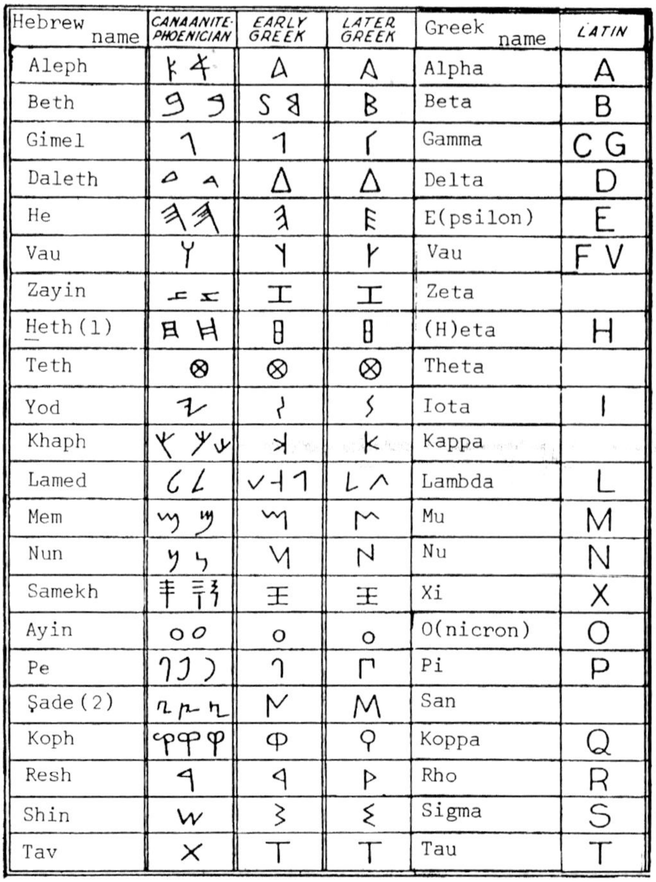

Hebrew name	CANAANITE PHOENICIAN	EARLY GREEK	LATER GREEK	Greek name	LATIN
Aleph	ﬡ ﬡ	Δ	A	Alpha	A
Beth	9 9	S ﬡ	B	Beta	B
Gimel	ﬤ	1	ſ	Gamma	C G
Daleth	◿ ◿	Δ	Δ	Delta	D
He	ﬡ ﬡ	ﬡ	E	E(psilon)	E
Vau	Y	Y	F	Vau	F V
Zayin	ﬡ ﬡ	I	I	Zeta	
Heth(1)	ﬡ ﬡ	ﬡ	ﬡ	(H)eta	H
Teth	⊗	⊗	⊗	Theta	
Yod	ﬡ	ﬡ	ﬡ	Iota	I
Khaph	ﬡ ﬡ	ﬡ	k	Kappa	
Lamed	ﬤ ﬤ	∨ �ꟷ ﬡ	L ∧	Lambda	L
Mem	ﬡ ﬡ	ﬡ	M	Mu	M
Nun	ﬡ ﬡ	ﬡ	N	Nu	N
Samekh	ﬡ ﬡ	ﬡ	ﬡ	Xi	X
Ayin	o o	o	o	O(nicron)	O
Pe	ﬡ ﬡ ﬡ	ﬡ	Γ	Pi	P
Şade (2)	ﬡ ﬡ ﬡ	ﬡ	M	San	
Koph	ﬡ ﬡ ﬡ	Φ	ﬡ	Koppa	Q
Resh	ﬡ	ﬡ	ﬡ	Rho	R
Shin	w	ﬡ	ﬡ	Sigma	S
Tav	X	T	T	Tau	T

(1) "H̲", commonly transliterated as "H" for simplicity, is pronounced in the Sumerian and Semitic languages as "CH" in the Scottish or German "loch".

(2) "Ş", commonly transliterated as "S" for simplicity, is pronounced in the Sumerian and Semitic languages as "TS".

Fig. 4

ALPHABET TABLE

Showing the letters of five non-Roman alphabets and the transliterations used in the etymologies

HEBREW[1,4]			ARABIC[3,4]					GREEK[7]		RUSSIAN[8]		SANSKRIT[11]		
א	aleph	', ʾ	ا	ل			alif	ʾ	A α alpha a		А a	a	अ a	ञ ñ
ב	beth	b, bh	ـب	ـبـ	ـ	ـ	bā	b	B β beta b		Б б	b	आ ā	ट ṭ
ג	gimel	g, gh	ـت	ـتـ	ـ	ـ	tā	t	Γ γ gamma g, n		В в	v	इ i	ठ ṭh
ד	daleth	d, dh	ـث	ـثـ	ـ	ـ	thā	th	Δ δ delta d		Г г	g	ई ī	ड ḍ
ה	he	h	ج	جـ	ـج	ـجـ	jīm	j	E ε epsilon e		Д д	d	उ u	ढ ḍh
ו	waw	w	ح	حـ	ـح	ـحـ	hā	ḥ	Z ζ zeta z		Е e	e	ऊ ū	ण ṇ
ז	zayin	z	خ	خـ	ـخ	ـخـ	khā	kh	Η η eta ē		Ж ж	zh	ऋ ṛ	त t
ח	heth	ḥ	د	ـد			dāl	d	Θ θ theta th		З э	z	ॠ ṝ	थ th
ט	teth	ṭ	ذ	ـذ			dhāl	dh	I ι iota i		И и Й й	i, ī	लृ ḷ	द d
י	yod	y	ر	ـر			rā	r	K κ kappa k		К к	k	लॄ ḹ	ध dh
כ ך	kaph	k, kh	ز	ـز			zāy	z	Λ λ lambda l		Л л	l	ए e	न n
ל	lamed	l	س	سـ	ـس	ـسـ	sīn	s	M μ mu m		М м	m	ऐ ai	प p
מ ם	mem	m	ش	شـ	ـش	ـشـ	shīn	sh	N ν nu n		Н н	n	ओ o	फ ph
נ ן	nun	n	ص	صـ	ـص	ـصـ	sād	ṣ	Ξ ξ xi x		О о	o	औ au	ब b
ס	samekh	s	ض	ضـ	ـض	ـضـ	dād	ḍ	O o omicron o		П п	p	ं ṃ	भ bh
ע	ayin	ʿ	ط	طـ	ـط	ـطـ	tā	ṭ	Π π pi p		Р р	r	ः ḥ	म m
פ ף	pe	p, ph	ظ	ظـ	ـظ	ـظـ	zā	ẓ	P ρ rho r, rh		С с	s	क k	य y
צ ץ	sadhe	ṣ	ع	عـ	ـع	ـعـ	ʿayn	ʿ	Σ σ ς sigma s		Т т	t	ख kh	र r
ק	qoph	q	غ	غـ	ـغ	ـغـ	ghayn	gh	T τ tau t		У у	u	ग g	ल l
ר	resh	r	ف	فـ	ـف	ـفـ	fā	f	Υ υ upsilon y, u		Ф ф	f	घ gh	व v
שׂ	sin	ś	ق	قـ	ـق	ـقـ	qāf	q	Φ φ phi ph		Х х	kh	ङ ṅ	श ś
שׁ	shin	sh	ك	كـ	ـك	ـكـ	kāf	k	X χ chi ch		Ц ц	ts	च c	ष ṣ
ת	taw	t, th	ل	لـ	ـل	ـلـ	lām	l	Ψ ψ psi ps		Ч ч	ch	छ ch	स s
			م	مـ	ـم	ـمـ	mīm	m	Ω ω omega ō		Ш ш	sh	ज j	ह h
			ن	نـ	ـن	ـنـ	nūn	n			Щ щ	shch		
			ه	هـ	ـه	ـهـ	hā	hʾ			Ъ ъ	"		
			و	ـو			wāw	w			Ы ы	y		
			ي	يـ	ـي	ـيـ	yā	y			Ь ь	'		
											Э э	e		
											Ю ю	yu		
											Я я	ya		

I am going to leave the Great Spacer and occupants some 1800 light-years from Earth. However, I can assure you that Billy Meier made it back home in Switzerland within the thirty hours that Semjase told him to make plans to be gone.

At this time I am going to quote some passages from the book *UFO...Contact From The Pleiades* and also show some of Billy Meier's amazing photographs (see these pictures in the photograph section).

Semjase: For the present, the Earth-human holds the weight of his destiny on his own shoulders. However, should a time arise where we would find it necessary to involve our-selves in certain matters pertaining to Earth, it would be done to prevent an aberration or possible cataclysm, that would effect the depths of Cosmic Space beyond the conscious thoughts of Earth-humans.

In other words, if we aren't smart enough, or maybe the right words aren't evolved enough to save ourselves, they aren't going to do it for us.

Ptaah: Thought transmission is the purest form of communication, as the conversation may not be manipulated into to something that it is not.

Semjase: A human may deliver himself from all ignorance if he generates the will to seek the truth.

Semjase: Enemies and attackers can only contribute to the growth of a spiritually developed person.

In the winter of 1975, Semjase gave Meier the most thorough explanation of the propulsion system to date. Two independent drives are necessary: normal drive and hyper-drive. The first, a "light-emitting device," permits safe navigation in or out of a system of planetary bodies and an acceleration of speed where they may then make the hyper-jump—a multi-process method of travel in which the object moves many times faster than the speed of light.

The Pleiadian stated that the mass of an object increases in relation to the speed that it travels, and here is where the first procedure of a hyper-space leap becomes a necessity. The ship is protected by the screens, which prevent the "mass speed correlation." When the energy field screens are withdrawn and the jump is made, the computers on board simultaneously accelerate the "essential distortion unit," which then creates dematerialization. Space and time become paralyzed as one, and in the instant it requires to create a thought, the beamship rematerializes at its destination.

Ptaah: The Earth-human interest in space is just beginning to awaken, but it will take a great deal to maintain the knowledge and discover the many secrets that await these pioneers.

Semjase: The Earth-human, who has consciously allowed himself to reason and think, has walked forward in steps of evolution. This day he has stepped out of this level and has gained greater reasoning and understanding. Evolution demands that he makes use of these forces but, indeed, they are only utilized to their full extent through spiritual development.

Semjase: When a being is happy, luck appears everywhere in his life because luck is a self-created state and comes from within the individual. It is a quality of the inner-being and an inseparable spark of the spirit that contains infinite force in its existence.

Semjase: Love is the instrument by which one may spread the internal force that can never be extinguished. It overcomes death and spreads light. It embodies the poise of wisdom, peace, and all that exceeds understanding.

Part Two

The Proof of Ancient Astronauts, Alias, Anunnaki, Nefilim, Elohim

Ninety-five percent of the credit for this part of the story belongs to Zecharia Sitchin. He has written the *Earth Chronicles*, a series of books dealing with Earth's and man's history and prehistories on the information in texts written down on clay tablets by the ancient civilizations of the Near East.

I would like to claim five percent of the story. Zecharia made nine exploratory expeditions to prove the things he had written about and I had the privilege of being on seven of them. He always had written a complete set of briefing notes, and on most nights on these ten-day expeditions he would have a meeting and go over the things we had seen. I also had the privilege of writing a newsletter that I believe gave me my five percent.

The following is Zecharia Sitchin's credentials. He was born in Russia and raised in Palestine, where he acquired a profound knowledge of modern and ancient Hebrew, other Semitic and European languages, the old testament, and the history and archaeology of the Near East. He attended the London School of Economics and Political Science and graduated from the University of London, majoring in economic history. He was a leading journalist and editor in Israel for many years. He is one of the few scholars able to read and understand Sumerian.

The Earth Chronicals: Time Chart
Events Before The Deluge

Years Ago

450,000   On Nibiru, a distant member of our solar system, life faces slow extinction as the planet's atmosphere erodes. Disposed by Anu, the ruler, Alalu escapes in a spaceship and finds refuge on Earth. He discovers that Earth has gold that can be used too protect Nibiru's atmosphere.

445,000   Led by Enki, son of Anu, the Anunnaki land on Earth, establish Eridu-Earth Station 1 for extracting gold from the waters of the Persian Gulf.

430,000   Earth's climate mellows. More Anunnaki arrive on Earth, among them Enki's half-sister Ninharsag, chief medical officer.

416,000   As gold production falters, Anu arrives on Earth with Enlil, the heir apparent. It is decided to obtain the vital gold by mining it in southern Africa. Drawing lots, Enlil wins command of Earth Mission; Enki is relegated to Africa.

            On departing Earth Anu is challenged by Alalu's grandson.

400,000   Seven functional settlements in southern Mesopotamia include a spaceport (Sippar), mission control center (Nippur), a metallurgical center (Badibira), and a medical center (Shuruppak).

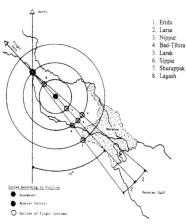

1. Eridu
2. Larsa
3. Nippur
4. Bad-Tibira
5. Larak
6. Sippar
7. Shuruppak
8. Lagash

| 400,000 | The ores arrive by ships from Africa: The refined metal is sent aloft to orbiters manned by Igigi, then transferred to spaceships arriving periodically from Nibiru. |

[See Baalbek photographs page 150]

| 380,000 | Gaining the support of the Igigi, Alalu's grandson attempts to seize mastery over Earth. The Enlilites win the war of the Olden Gods. |
| 300,000 | The Anunnaki toiling in the mines mutiny. Enki and Ninharsag create Primitive Worker through genetic manipulation of Apewoman. They take over the manual chores of the Anunnaki. Enlil raids the mines, brings the Primitive Workers to the Edin in Mesopotamia. Given the ability to procreate, *Homo sapiens* begin to multiply. |

Excerpts from the Sitchin Study Newsletter
APRIL 1998

The Cast Of Players
ENKI [EA] Son of Anu—Chief Scientist
NINHARSHAG [NINTI] half-sister of Enki—The Birth Goddess
ANUNNAKI [NEFILIM] [ELOHIM]
ADAPA—[THE ADAM] [THE LULU] —*Homo sapiens*
ADAM—The Biblical Man

The Scenario
The Anunnaki came to Earth to obtain gold (it was probably needed to help their home planet's atmosphere). From the ocean, this failed. Next they went to the ABZU in the lower world, which means they went to southern Africa. The Mesopotamian texts (clay tablets) tell it like this: "*In the distant sea, 100 Beru of water (away)...the ground of Arali(is)...It is where the Blue stones cause ill...Where the craftmans of Anu, the silver axe carries, which shines as the day.*" One hundred beru is believed to be two hundred hours of sailing; this would be two thousand to three thousand miles to southern Africa. After some 150,000 years of hard toil in the underground mines, the Anunnaki workers mutinied.

The Solution

To solve this problem, it was decided to try to genetically produce a primitive worker. The "being" was available, but Homo erectus posed a problem. On one hand, he was too intelligent and wild to become simply a docile beast of work. On the other hand, he was not really suited to the task. His physique had to be changed. He had to be able to grasp and use the tools of the Anunnaki, walk and bend like them so that he could replace the Anunnaki in the fields and mines. He had to have better "brains"—not like the Anunnaki but enough to understand speech and commands and the task allotted to him.

The tale's baffling details may hold an important truth. It's quite conceivable that before resorting to the creation of a being in their own image, the Nefilim attempted to come up with a "manufactured servant" by experimenting with other alternatives: the creation of a hybrid ape-man animal. Some of these artificial creatures may have survived for a while but were certainly unable to reproduce. Enigmatic bull-men and lion-men (sphinxes) that adorned temple sights in the ancient New East may not have been just figments of an artist's imagination but actual creatures that came as the biological laboratories of the Nefilim—unsuccessful experiments commemorated in art and statutes.

THE 12TH PLANET
(C) Z. SITCHIN

Sumerian text, too, speaks of deformed humans created by Enki and the Mother Goddess (Ninharsag) in the course of their efforts to fashion a perfect primitive worker. One text reports that Ninharsag produced a man who could not hold back his urine, a woman who could not bear children, a being who had neither male nor female organs. All in all, six deformed or deficient humans were brought forth by Ninharsag. Enki was held responsible for the imperfect creations of humans with diseased eyes, trembling hands, a sick liver, a failing heart; others with sicknesses attendant to old age; and so on.

But finally the perfect man was achieved—the one Enki named Adapa: The Bible named him Adam; our scholars named him *Homo sapien*. This being was so much akin to the gods that one text even went so far as to point out that the Mother Goddess gave to her creature, man, "a skin as the skin of a god"—a smooth hairless body, quite different from that of the shaggy ape-man.

With this final product, Nefilim were genetically compatible with the daughters of man and able to marry them and have children by them. But such compatibility could exist only if man had developed from the "same seed of life" as the Nefilim. This indeed is what the ancient text attests.

In a parallel old Babylon text named "Creation of Man by the Mother Goddess," the gods called upon "the Midwife of the Gods, the Knowing Mami" and tell her:

Thou art the mother-womb
The one Mankind can create.
Create then Lulu, let him bear the yoke!

At this point, the text "When Gods as Men" and the parallel text turn to a detailed description of the actual creation of man. Accepting the "job," the goddess (she being named NINTI—"lady who gives life") spelled out some requirements, including some chemicals ("bitumens of the Abzu") to be used for "purification," and "the clay of the Abzu."

Whatever these materials were, Ea/Enki had no problem understanding the requirements. Accepting, he said:

I will prepare a purifying bath.
Let one god be bled....
From his flesh and blood
let Ninti mix the clay.

To shape a man from the mixed clay, some feminine assistance—some pregnancy or childbearing aspects—were also needed. Enki offered the services of his own spouse.

Ninki, my goddess-spouse,
will be the one for labor

Seven goddesses-of-birth
will be near, to assist

Ninki blessed the new being and presented him to Ea. Some cylinder seals (amazingly sophisticated small rollers with the picture carved in reverse so as to make a positive picture when rolled on wet clay (a technology that had to be taught to mankind by the Anunnaki) show a goddess, flanked by the tree of life and laboratory flasks, holding up a newborn being.

The being that was produced, which is repeatedly referred to in Mesopotamian text as a "model man" or a "mold," was apparently the right creature, for the gods too clamored for duplicates. This seemingly unimportant detail, however, throws light not only on the process by which mankind was "created," but also on the otherwise conflicting information contained in the Bible. According to the first chapter of Genesis:

Elomin created the Adam in his image—
in the image of Elomin created him.

Chapter 5, which is called the Book of genealogies of Adam, states that:

On the day that Elomin created Adam,
in the likeness of Elomin did he make him.
Male and female created he them,
and he blessed them, and called them "Adam"
on the very day of their creation.

In the same breath, we are told that the deity created, in his likeness and his image, only a single being, "the Adam," and in apparent contradiction, that both a male and a female were created simultaneously. The contradiction seems sharper still in the second chapter of Genesis, which specifically reports that the Adam was alone for awhile, until the Deity put him to sleep and fashioned Woman from a rib.

The contradiction, which has puzzled scholars and theologians alike, disappears once we realize that the biblical texts were a condensation of the original Sumerian sources. These sources inform that after trying to fashion a primitive worker by "mixing" apeman with animals, the god concluded at the only mixture that would work would be between apeman and the Nefilim and themselves. After several unsuccessful attempts, a "model"—Adapa/Adam—was made. There was, at first, only a single Adam.

Once Adapa/Adam proved to be the right creature, he was used as the genetic model or "mold" for the creation of duplicates, and those duplicates were not only male, but male and female. As we showed earlier, the biblical "rib" from which Woman was fashioned was a play on words on the Sumerian TI ("rib" and "life"), confirming that Eve was made of Adam's life essence.

The Mesopotamian texts provided us with an eyewitness report of the first production of the duplicates of Adam.

The instructions of Enki were followed. In the house of Shimti—where the breath of life is "blown in"—Enki, the Mother Goddess, and fourteen birth goddesses assembled. A god's "essence" was obtained, the "purifying bath" prepared. Ea cleaned the clay in her presence; he kept reciting incantations.

The god who purifies the Naishtu, Ea spoke up
Seated before her, he was prompting her,
After she had recited her incantations,
She put a hand out to the clay.

We are now privy to the detailed process of man's mass creation. With fourteen birth goddesses present:

Ninti nipped off fourteen pieces of clay;
seven she deposited on the right
Seven she placed on the left.
Between them she placed the mould.

...the hair she...
...the cutter of the umbilical cord.

[The dotted lines denote unreadable words on the clay tablets.]
It is evident that the birth goddesses were divided into two groups. "The wise and learned, twice-seven birth goddesses had assembled," the text goes on to explain. Into their wombs the Mother Goddess deposited the "clay mix." There are hints of a surgical procedure—the removal or shaving off of hair, readying of a surgical instrument, a cutter. Now there was nothing to do but wait.

The birth goddesses were kept together.
Ninti sat counting the months.
The fateful tenth month was approaching;
The tenth month arrived;
The period of opening the womb had elapsed.
Her face radiated understanding:
She covered her head, performed the midwifery.
Her waist she girdled, pronounced the blessing.
She drew a shape, in the mold was life.

The drama of man's creation, it appears, was compounded by a late birth. The "mixture" of "clay" and "blood" was used to induce pregnancy in fourteen birth goddesses. But nine months passed, and the tenth month commenced. "The period of opening the womb had elapsed." Understanding what was called for, the Mother Goddess "performed the midwifery." That she engaged in some surgical operation emerged more clearly from a parallel text (in spite of its fragmentation):

Ninti...counts the month...
The destined tenth month they called;
The lady whose hand opens came.
With the...she opened the womb.
Her face brightened with joy.
Her head was covered;
...made an opening;
That which was in the womb came forth.

Overcome with joy, the Mother Goddess let out a cry: "I have created! *My hands have made it!*" (from *The 12th Planet* by Zecharia Sitchin.)

The Garden of Eden
The saga of mankind's creation, according to Sitchin, did not end with the "artful creation" of a lulu by Enki and Ninharsag some 300,000 years ago. As a hybrid, the new being could not procreate (just as a mule, a hybrid between a horse and a she-ass, cannot procreate); the need for primitive workers far exceeded the slow process of employing "birth goddesses" to proved them, even (as the Sumerian text states) in "batches of seven."

So Enki resorted to a second feat of genetic engineering: He provided the new beings with the ability to procreate by adding to their twenty-two pairs of chromosomes the male "x" and "y" ones, thereby enabling them to have offspring.

This feat, according to Sitchin in *Genesis Revisited*, is recalled in the biblical tale of Adam and Eve in the Garden of Eden. As the tale indicates, until Eve and Adam ate the fruit of "knowing" they did not even realize that they were naked; only after did they cover their genitals. Expelled from the Garden of Eden, they started to procreate. "And Adam knew his wife Eve." (In the biblical Hebrew, "to know" in this context meant to have sex for procreational purposes.)

In his writings, Sitchin dwells on the identity of the "Serpent" that initiated the sexual transformation, and the meaning of the term both in Hebrew and in the original Sumerian text, and shows that it referred to Enki in his role as a biologist and master of the secrets of DNA and genetics.

200,000	Life on Earth regresses during a new glacial period.
100,000	Climate warms again. The Anunnaki (the biblical Nefilim), to Enlil's growing annoyance, marry the daughters of man.
75,000	The "accusation of Earth"—a new ice age—begins. Regressive type of man roam the Earth. Cro-Magnon man survives.
49,000	Enki and Ninharsag elevate humans of Anunnaki parentage to rule in Shuruppak. Enlil, enraged, plots mankind's demise.
13,000	Realizing that the passage of Nibiru in Earth's proximity will trigger an immense tidal wave, Enlil makes the Anunnaki swear to keep the impending calamity a secret from Mankind.

B.C. II Events After The Deluge

11,000	Enki breaks the oath, instructs Ziusudra/Noah to build a submersible ship. The deluge sweeps over the Earth; the Anunnaki witness the total destruction from orbiting spacecraft.
10,500	The descendants of Noah are allotted three regions. Ninurta, Enlil's foremost son, dams the mountains and drains the rivers to make Mesopotamia habitable; Enki reclaims the Nile Valley. The Sinai peninsula is retained by the Anunnaki for a post-Diluvial spaceport: A control center is established on Mount Moriah (the future Jerusalem).

After the Great Flood, the Anunnaki had to have a different spaceport because the one in Mesopotamia was under water and mud. The new spaceport was laid out with an accuracy that any Earth-bound *Homo sapien* was incapable of achieving.

The new spaceport alignments are shown on page 128 Using Mount Ararat as the starting point two 11.5-degree angles were laid out; one side went through Baalbek to a point on the thirtieth parallel where the Anunnaki built the pyramids of Ginza.

(See picture of 1200-ton cut stone at Baalbek, Lebanon on page 150.)

The pyramids of Giza and the Sphinx were built by the Anunnaki on the thirtieth parallel with the Sphinx looking east on the thirtieth parallel toward the spaceport.

The spaceport was located in the Sinai on the thirtieth parallel on a line from Mount Ararat through Mission Control Center. Mission Control has some of the most compelling Anunnaki evidence as it was built on a massive cut stone platform. It contained several cut stones that weighed 500 to 600 tons each. Sitchin has dated these constructions to approximately 9000 B.C. some 11000 years ago. (See the photograph taken in the so-called tunnel on Sitchin's expedition to the holy land, September 1997.)

Many years later, when *Homo sapiens* multiplied and inhabited the area it became known as Jerusalem, a focal point of the Jewish, Moslem, and Christian religions.

(See picture of 500 to 600 ton cut stone on page 151.)

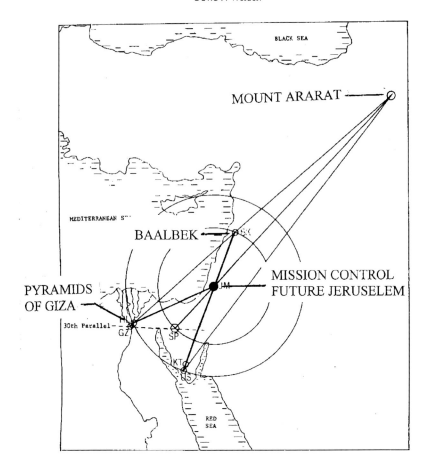

9,780	Ra/Marduk, Enki's firstborn son, divides dominion over Egypt between Osiris and Seth.
9,300	Seth seizes and dismembers Osiris. Assumes sole rule over the Nile Valley.
8,970	Horus avenges his father Osiris by launching the First Pyramid War.

Seth escapes to Asia, seizes the Sinai peninsula and Canaan.

| 8,670 | Opposed to the resulting control of all the space facilities of Enki's descendants, the Enlilites launch the Second Pyramid War. The victorious Ninurta empties the Great Pyramid of its equipment. |

Sitchin Study Newsletter

Proof No. 1 that the pharaohs did not build the Pyramids of Giza.

Early in the first century A.D. the Roman geographer and historian Strabo entered into the Great Pyramid through an opening in the north face, hidden by a hinged stone. Going down a long narrow passage, he reached a pit dug in the bedrock—as other Greek and Roman tourists had done before him.

The location of this entryway was forgotten when in 820 A.D. Moslem Caliph Al Mamoon attempted to enter the pyramid. Blasting through the mass of stones by heating and cooling them until they cracked, by ramming and chiseling, Al Mamoon's men advanced inch by inch. They were about to give up when they heard the sound of a falling stone ahead, indicating that some cavity was located there. The end result was the discovery of a secret entrance to an ascending passageway.

The Pharaohs built all of the other pyramids before 820 A.D. and copied the Great Pyramid; however, they did not know about the secret entrance to the ascending passageway. Consequently, none of the Pharaoh-built pyramids contained an ascending passageway.

The dotted line shows the passageway that Al Mamoon took as he

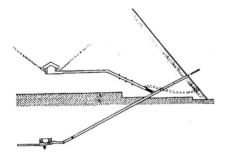

blasted through the Great Pyramid, ending with the discovery of the ascending passageway

Proof No. 2 that the pharaohs did not build the Pyramids of Giza

The Mass and the Precision of the Great Pyramid
Though the Second Pyramid is only slightly smaller than the first "Great Pyramid" (height: 470 and 480 feet: sides at base 707 and 756 feet, respectively), it is the latter that has by and large captured the interest and

imagination of scholars and laymen since men set their eyes on these monuments. It has been and still remains the largest stone building in the world, having been constructed of an estimated 2,300,000 to 2,500,000 slabs of yellow limestone (the core), white limestone (the smooth facing or casing), and granite (for interior chambers and galleries, for roofing, etc.). Its total mass, estimated at some 93 million cubic feet weighing 7 million tons, has been calculated to exceed that of all the cathedrals, churches, and chapels that have been built in England since the beginning of Christianity.

"Remo! Lift with your knees, not your back!"

The white limestone casing stones were removed in Arab times and used for the construction of nearby Cairo; but a few can be seen near the top of the second pyramid, and some were discovered at the base of the Great Pyramid. The casing stones are the heaviest of all the stones used to build the pyramid proper. The six faces that each stone has have been cut and polished to an accuracy of optical standards—they fit not only the core stones that they covered, but also each other on all four sides, forcing a precision-made area of twenty-one acres of limestone blocks.

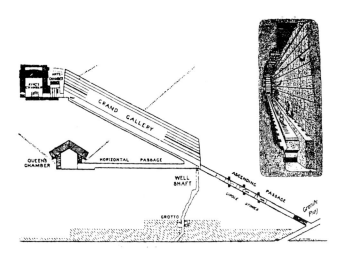

These pictures show the so-called King and Queen Chambers and The Grand Gallery, a part of the ascending passageway in the Great Pyramid. It is a technical masterpiece of precision cut and placed granite and limestone. It is highly questionable if the feat of building this pyramid could be done by modern day *Homo sapiens*, let alone the early Egyptian *Homo sapiens*. There are no pharaoh-built pyramids that can come close to the mass and precision of the pyramids of Giza. Zecharia Sitchin has suggested that the Giza pyramids and the Sphinx were erected by the Anunnaki in connection with the new spaceport in the Sinai, some 11,000 years ago.

What the Egyptologists Say

The suggestion that the Giza pyramids were built at such an early time, and by extraterrestrials to boot, is—to put it mildly—not what Egyptologists have been saying and teaching.

Open any textbook on the subject, and you will read that all of Egypt's pyramids—some twenty-odd main ones—were built by a succession of pharaohs as glorified tombs for themselves. The first one, you read, was built by a king called Zoser, the second of the pharaohs of the Third Dynasty, circa 2650 B.C. The practice, we are told, was continued by the three renowned pharaohs of the Fourth Dynasty—Khufu (Chcops in Greek) built the Great Pyramid; Chefra (Chefren) the second pyramid; and their successor Menkara (Mycerinus) the third one—all in less than a century, circa 2500 B.C. It was Chefren who had carved out the Sphinx, according to textbooks. Then subsequent pharaohs raised their own pyramid-tombs at various other Egyptian sites.

How do Egyptologists know all that? In the various pyramids other than Giza, hieroglyphic inscriptions name the pharaohs by or for whom they were built. They are profusely decorated, and the walls are covered with verses from the Book of the Dead, in which the pharaoh's name has been inscribed as the one to be welcomed by the gods in his afterlife. The three pyramids of Giza are different, not only in the immense size of the two of them and their incredible durability, or inner complexity (especially the Great Pyramid). They are different also in that they are totally devoid of any decoration, any inscription, any quotation. So how do Egyptologists know who built them and the Sphinx?

First, simply by saying that successive pharaohs built pyramids, those of Giza ought to have "belonged" to the three of the fourth Dynasty (most other pyramids are from the Sixth Dynasty). Second, at one time archaeologists had identified within the smaller pyramid a wooden coffin with some skeletal remains, and on the coffin the pharaoh's name, Men-Ka-Ra, was spelled out. Third, in some narrow spaces called relieving chambers within the Great Pyramid, the name of Khufu (Cheops) was found painted in red by ancient stone masons.

So, by a process of elimination, the second pyramid had to be built by the pharaoh who reigned between them, i.e., Chefra (Chefren) as well as the Sphinx, carving on its face his own royal image. Since Herodotus appears to suggest the same attributions in his description of Egypt, Egyptologists have adhered to these identifications as gospel.

What Zecharia Sitchin Says

Sumerian texts, about whose antiquity and authenticity there is no question, relate not only the events of the Deluge but also what ensued. In those texts (from sources amply listed in Sitchin's books) the mounting conflicts among the leaders of the Anunnaki are recorded. Several times the conflicts erupted into full-scale warfare; he dubbed the bitterest ones (in the third book The War of Gods and Men) "The Pyramid Wars" because they involved the Giza pyramids. As the epithet suggests, the pyramids of Giza had already existed when these conflicts were occurring—millennia before there were paranoiac rulers in Egypt.

Indeed, one long text (well known to Orientalists) describes how the victorious leader of a Mesopotamian clan, having vanquished the African clan, entered the Great Pyramid and destroyed or removed its pulsating crystals and humming instruments, also toppling its apex stone (which has been missing since). By his calculations, this happened 6,000 years before Khufu's time!

If Sumerian sources conflicted with Egyptological dogma, what about ancient Egyptian sources? Examining them, Sitchin also found problems with current view. There is, for example, a famous stela (on exhibit in the Cairo Museum). It is known as the Inventory Stela, which is inscribed by the very Khufu (Cheops) to whom the Great Pyramid is attributed. The inscription commemorated the completion of a temple to the Goddess Isis that Khufu had built. He called Isis "Mistress of the Pyramid" and states that he built the temple "beside the House of the Sphinx."

"I read and reread the inscription," Sitchin wrote. "Did I really understand what it implied?" The textbooks say that it was Chefren, who had reigned after Khufu, who had built (or carved out) the Sphinx, with his image as its face. So how could his predecessor build a temple to Isis beside the Sphinx if it was not yet carved out?

I have discovered that some of the most archaic Egyptian tablets already depict the Sphinx. The great Egyptologist Sir Flinders Petrie, in his masterwork The Royal Tombs of the Earliest Dynasties (1901) attributed the Sphinx to a pre-dynasty king centuries before Cheops.

The Third Pyramid Fraud

Sitchin continued to state in his writing: It was obviously necessary to verify the two concrete pieces of evidence in the hands of Egyptologists—the coffin lid inscribed Men-Ka-Ra from the third pyramid, and the red paint markings spelling out Khufu's name in the Great Pyramid.

Tracing the information from textbooks to an earlier one, which relied on previous textbooks and so on backward, I came across an interesting puzzle: At some point, the initial references to the coffin lid evidence somehow began to disappear from the later textbooks.

Why?

With considerable effort, I found out why. Using modern dating methods, subsequent research established that the coffin lid was from a much later dynasty, which also had a ruler named Menkara, and the skeletal bones were from millennia later, from a Christian burial.

In other words, someone had perpetrated a deliberate fraud, bringing a piece of wooden coffin from another tomb and bones from a Christian-era grave into the pyramid and saying, "Hey, look what I found." And so, realizing the fraud, Egyptologists finally dropped the claim to proof of the third pyramid builder's identity.

Who had perpetrated this fraud? He was a British Colonel by the name of Howard Vyse, a black sheep of a prominent family who was sent away to cruise the Mediterranean and ended up infatuated with Egyptian antiquities. The year was 1835, and it was the time when new finds in Egypt made their discoverer world famous. Enlisting some dubious assistants, including a Mr. Hill, Vyse embarked on searches within Giza pyramids. Hungry for some memorable achievements, he engineered (or acquiesced in) the pyramid fraud.

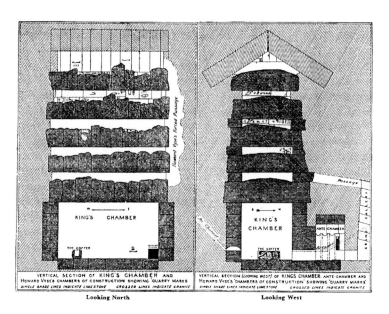

Looking North   Looking West

134

The Great Pyramid Fraud

The pretended search within the smaller pyramid was only a side show. Vyse's main work, lasting into mid-1837, was inside the Great Pyramid. He described his day-by-day efforts, problems, and frustrations in a detailed journal that he kept.

Not able to find anything of significance, he resorted to the use of gun powder inside the ancient and unique monument to force his way into unknown parts above the so-called King's Chamber. Above a then-known space called Davison's Chamber he found other spaces that are now called relieving chambers. He named the first one after Lord Wellington, and had his assistant Mr. Hill inscribe the name inside the narrow chamber with red paint.

Additional chambers were then entered, without anything to cheer about. Inscribed in red paint were "quarry marks," as well as cartouches spelling out royal names.

In his journal, Vyse provided a drawing showing a schematic of the various chambers where the inscribed markings were found.

The news was rushed to Cairo, and the British and Austrian consuls were invited to witness the finds. Mr. Hill made a facsimile of the cartouches on cloth-lined paper, and all present authenticated it. The document was then sent the British Museum in London, and the event made great news, because the discovered cartouches spelled out the name of Khufu—in chambers that have been sealed since the pyramids have been built.

Khufu was certified, in writing, to have been the builder of the Great Pyramid; and so it has remained stated in all the textbooks.

The Great Fraud

But researching the reports from that time, 150 years ago, I found that several leading Egyptologists of the time, including the curator at the British Museum, had doubts regarding the cartouches. The writing and spelling seemed wrong.

After great efforts and initial claims by the officials in the museum that no such document existed, they found and let me examine the "Hill Facsimile." As I unrolled the sheet, I at once knew that it was all a fraud, a forgery. Whoever had written the royal name had misspelled it. Instead of writing Kh-u-fu he used the hieroglyphic symbols spelling out Ra-u-fu.

Since Ra was the name of the supreme god of ancient Egypt, the improper use of his name was blasphemy. No ancient scribe would have dared to do it. It could have been done only by someone not fully cognizant with ancient Egyptian writing.

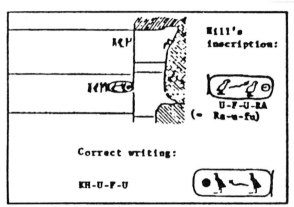

Cartouche showing incorrect and correct hieroglyphic spelling of Khufu's name

In *The Stairway to Heaven*, I identified the culprit as Mr. Hill, suggesting the night of May 28, 1837, as the time when he had entered the pyramid with a brush and red paint and simulated the royal name.

The Great Pyramid discovery was only a great fraud, I concluded. There has been no real evidence for identifying the Giza pyramids with any pharaoh as their builder. Therefore, the other Sumerian and Egyptian evidence was valid; the Anunnaki were their builders—millennia before Cheops and Chefren and Mycerinus.

An Unexpected Eyewitness

Three years after *The Stairway to Heaven* was published, in May 1983, I found in the mail a letter from a Mr. Walter M. Allen of Pittsburgh. "I have read your book," he wrote. "What you say about the forgery in the Cheops Pyramid was not new to me." His great-grandfather, he wrote, was an eyewitness to the forgery.

"I have your letter of May 7 and I am literally flabbergasted," I wrote him back. "That my conclusion could be supported by a virtual eyewitness was beyond my wildest expectation!"

As the story unfolded, with some family documents shown to me, it turned out that Mr. Allen's great-grandfather was the very stonemason from England whom Col. Vyse had engaged to use gunpowder inside the pyramid. On that particular night, he had witnessed Mr. Hill go into the pyramid with red paint and a brush, supposedly to paint over ancient markings but actually to paint new ones.

When the great-grandfather objected, he was fired and banned from the site. He reported all that in letters regularly written to his father in Box, Wiltshire, in England. When the family moved to the United States, the family records were brought over. Mr. Allen became aware of it all when he began to write down the family's history by interviewing the still-living relatives.

The name, the circumstances, the dates—all that I had surmised was exactly corroborated by the Allen family records.

The Sphinx Speaks Up

In 1991 a scientific paper presented at the convention of the Geological Society of America, held in San Diego, made worldwide headlines such as this one in the October 23rd *Los Angeles Times*: SPHINX NEW RIDDLE—IS IT OLDER THAN THE EXPERTS SAY?

The headlines referred to a report by Dr. Robert M. Schoch, a geologist at Boston University, and Dr. Thomas L. Dobecki, a Houston-based geophysicist, that patterns of water erosion on the Sphinx and other meteorological data indicate "that the Sphinx has been standing since before the Giza plateau became desert, 7000 B.C. or earlier."

"I am trying to be conservative," Dr. Dobecki said about the Sphinx's age in an interview with the *Los Angeles Times* science editor.

In March of 1992, the American Association for the Advancement of Science devoted a session to the subject "How old is the Sphinx?" at its annual meeting in Chicago.

The presentation by Dobecki and Schoch was vehemently objected to by certain Egyptologists. "You don't overthrow Egyptian history based on one phenomenon, like a weathering profile," one objector argued.

In June of 1992 *The New York Times* published an article by Anthony West, who started meteorological research, which presented forensic evidence that the face of the Sphinx in no way showed the features of the Pharaoh Chefren, as Egyptologists have been asserting. Sitchin took the opportunity to point out in a letter to the editor that his own estimate for the age of the Sphinx (about 9000 B.C.) was presented in his 1976 and 1980 books.

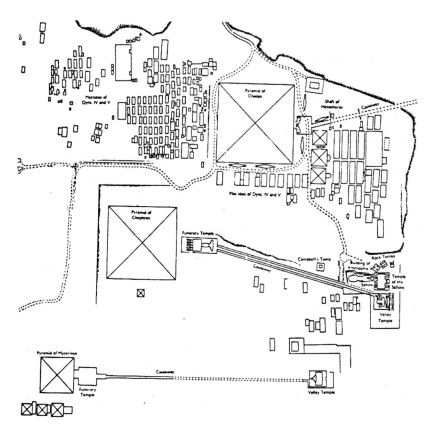

More proof that the pharoahs did not build the Pyramids of Giza

The three Pyramids of Giza are surrounded by smaller pyramids, satellite pyramids, temples, mastabas tombs. Though attributed to different rulers, the three obviously were planned and executed as a cohesive group, perfectly aligned not only to the cardinal points of the compass but also with one another. It has already been proven that the Sphinx is at least 9000 years old, and because The Pyramid of Giza and the Sphinx were planned and executed as a cohesive group, they are also at least 9000 years old.

8,670	Ninharhag, half sister of Enki and Enlil, convenes a peace conference. The division of Earth is reaffirmed. Rule over Egypt transferred from Ra/Marduk dynasty to that of Thoth. Heliopolis built as a substitute Beacon City.
8,500	The Anunnaki establish outpost at the gateway to the space facilities; Jerico is one of them.
7,400	As era of peace continues, the Anunnaki grant mankind new advances; the Neolithic period begins; Demigods rule over Egypt.
3,800	Urban civilization begins in Sumer as the Anunnaki reestablish the olden cities, beginning with Eridu and Nippur.

The Sudden Civilization

In 1919, H. R. Hall came upon ancient ruins at a village now called El-Ubaid. The site gave its name to what scholars now consider the first phase of the great Sumerian civilization. Sumerian cities of that period—ranging from northern Mesopotamia to the southern Zagro foothills—produced the first use of clay bricks, plastered walls, mosaic decorations, cemeteries with brick lined graves, painted and decorated ceramic wares with geometric designs, copper mirrors, beads of imported turquoise, paint for eyelids, copper headed "tomahawks," cloth, houses, and, above all, monumental temple buildings.

Farther south, the archaeologists found Eridu—the first sumerian city, according to ancient texts. As the excavators dug deeper, they came upon a temple dedicated to Enki, Sumer's God of Knowledge, which appeared to have been built and rebuilt many times over. The strata clearly led the scholars back to the beginnings of the Sumerian civilization: 2500 B.C., 2800 B.C., 3000 B.C., 3500 B.C.

Then the spades came upon the foundations of the first temple dedicated to Enki. Below that, there was virgin soil—nothing had been built before. The time was circa 3800 B.C. That is when civilization began.

It was not only the first civilization in the true sense of the term. It was a most extensive civilization, all-encompassing, in many ways more advanced than the other ancient cultures that had followed it. It was undoubtedly the civilization on which our own is based.

Having begun to use stone tools some 2,000,000 years earlier, man achieved this unprecedented civilization in Sumer circa 3800 B.C. and the perplexing fact about this is that to this very day the scholars have no inkling who the Sumerians were, where they came from, and how and why their civilization appeared.

For its appearance was sudden, unexpected, and out of nowhere.

H. Frankford (tell Uqair) called it "astonishing." Pierre Amiet (Elam) termed it "extraordinary." A. Parrot (Sumer) described it as "a flame which blasted up so suddenly." Leo Oppenheim (ancient Mesopotamia) stressed "the astonishingly short period" within which this civilization had arisen. Joseph Campbell (*The Masks of God*) summed it up this way: "with stunning abruptness...there appears in this little mud garden...the whole cultural syndrome that has since contributed the germinal unit of all the high civilizations of the world."

3800	Anu comes to Earth for a pageantful visit. A new city, Eruk (Ereck), is built in his honor. He makes the temple the abode of his beloved granddaughter Inanna/Ishtar.
B.C.	III Kingship on Earth
3760	Mankind granted kingship. Kish is the first capital under the aegis of Ninurta. The calendar is begun at Nippur. Civilization blossoms out in Sumer (the First Region).
3450	Primacy in Sumer transferred to Nanar/Sin. Marduk proclaims Babylon "Gateway of the Gods." "The Tower of Babel" incident. The Anunnaki confuse mankind's languages. His coup frustrated. Marduk/Ra returns to Egypt, deposes Thoth. Seizes his younger brother Dumuzi, who had berothed Inanna. Dumuzi accidentally killed; Marduk imprisoned alive in the Great Pyramid. Freed through an emergency shaft, he goes into exile.
3100	350 years of chaos ends with the installation of Egyptian Pharaoh in Memphis. Civilization comes to the Second Region.
2900	Kingship in Sumer transferred to Erech. Inanna given dominion over the Third Region; the Indus Valley civilization begins.
2650	Sumer's royal capital shifts about. Kingship deteriorates. Enlil loses patience with the unruly human multitudes.
2371	Inanna falls in love with Sharru-Kin (Sargon). He estab-

lishes new capital city. Agade (AKKad) Akkadian empire launched.

2316   Aiming to rule the Four Regions, Sargon removes sacred soil from Babylon. The Marduk-Inanna conflict flares again. It ends when Nergal, Marduk's brother, Journeys from South Africa to Babylon and persuades Marduk to leave Mesopotamia.

2291   Naram-sin ascends the throne of Akkad. Directed by the war-like Inanna, he penetrates the Sinai Peninsula, invades Egypt.

2255   Inanna usurps the power in Mesopotamia; Naram-Sim defiles Nippur. The Great Anunnaki obliterate Agade. Inanna escapes. Sumer and Akkad occupied by foreign troops loyal to Enlil and Ninuta.

2193   Terah, Abraham's father, born in Nippur into a priestly-royal family.

2180   Egypt divided: followers of Ra/ Marduk retain the south; Pharaohs opposed to him gain the throne of lower Egypt.

2130   As Enlil and Ninurta are increasingly away, central authority also deteriorates in Mesopotamia. Inanna's attempt to regain the Kingship for Erech does not last.

B.C.   IV The Fateful Century
2123   Abraham born in Nippur.
2113   Enlil entrusts the lands of Shem to Nammu, ascends the throne, is named protector of Nippur. A Nippurian priest-Terah, Abraham's father, comes to Ur to liaison with its royal court.

2096   Ur-Nammu dies in battle. The people consider his untimely death a betrayal by Anu and Enlil. Terah departs with his family for Harran.

2095   Shulgi ascends the throne of Ur, strengthens immoral ties. As empire thrives, Shulgi falls under charms of Inanna, becomes her lover. Grants Larsa to Elamites in exchange for serving as his Foreign Legion.

2080   Theban princes loyal to Ra/Marduk press northward under Mentohotep I. Nabu Marduk's son gains adherents for his father in Western Asia.

2055	On Nannar's orders, Shulgi send Elamite troops to suppress unrest in Canaanite cities. Elamites reach the gateway to the Sinia peninsula and its spaceport.
2048	Shulgi dies. Marduk moves to the land of the Hitties. Abraham ordered to southern Canaan with an elite corps of cavalrymen.
2047	Amar-Sin (the biblical Amarphel) becomes King of Ur. Abraham goes to Egypt, stays five years, then returns with more troops.
2041	Guided by Inanna, Amar-Sin forms a coalition of King of the East, launches military expedition to Caanan and Sinai. Its leader is the Elamite Khedorla's omer. Abraham blocks the advance at the gateway to the spaceport.
2038	Slui-Sin replaces Amar-Sin on the throne of Ur as the empire disintegrates.
2029	Ibbi-Sin replaces Shu-Sin. The western provinces tilt increasingly to Marduk.
2024	Leading his followers, Marduk marches on Sumer, enthrones himself in Babylon. Fighting spreads to central Mesopotamia, Nippur's holy of Holies is defiled, Enlil demands punishment for Marduk and Nabu; Enki opposes, but his son Hergal sides with Enlil. As Nabu marshals his Canaanite followers to capture the spaceport, the Great Anunnaki approves the use of nuclear weapons. Nergal and Ninurta destroy the spaceport and the errant Canaanite cities.
2023	The winds carry the radioactive cloud to Sumer, people die a terrible death. Animals perish, the water is poisoned, the soil becomes barren. Sumer and its great civilization lie prostrate. Its legacy passes to Abraham's seed as he begets—at age 100—a legitimate heir, Isaac.

Travis Walton: The monstrous trio of humanoids started toward me, their hands reach out at me.

Travis Walton: A real human type person shows up while Travis was in the control room with the stars showing through the transparent walls. The real human person with the sandy-blond hair, has many of the same characteristics as the normal-looking man that Kathie meets in the Rough River State Park and as Semjase, the Pleiadian.

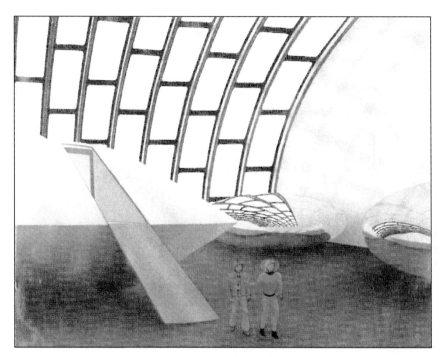

Travis Walton: The side walls of the passage outside the door sloped down at a 45 degree angle to meet a ramp that continued to slope downward. I was in a huge room. The room was shaped like one quarter of a cylinder laid on its side.

Many cigar shaped mother-ships have been seen and I believe that is what this is.

Travis Walton: The Return – as I raised my head up, a white light caught my eye just before it blinked off. Then I saw only the mirrored outline of a silvery disc hovering 4 feet above the paved surface of the road.

3 March, 1975 10:00 hours

Location: Jacobsberg-Allenberg, Switzerland
The four ships, two seven meter variations and two five meter remote
class, pass overhead.

The one armed man, Billy Meier and landing tracks.

26 March 1981
Location: Sekar Durchstolen, Switzerland

This photograph marked the first photo session allowed by the
Pleiadians since 1976. The five year moratorium on "photo proofs" was
enacted due to their concern of Meiers welfare and the repeated misuse
and abuse of the original photographs. Over eight hundred were taken
between 1975 and 1976, but only a few remain today. This new
beamship, designated Variation V1, is the most advanced from Pleiadian
technology. It has many new features including propultion that allows it
to make the hyper-jump between the Pleiades and Earth in seven minutes, instead of the old time travel of seven hours.

Fritz Meyer "holds up" a 1200 ton cut stone with one hand on Sitchin's exploratory trip to Syria and Lebanon.

August 1998
For reasons unknown, this megalithic cut stone was never moved from the quarry to the Great Platform three quarters of a mile away. The location of the five million square foot platform can be identified by the rows of columns in the background. Located in a special area in the mountains of Lebanon, many Roman rulers, over a period of four centuries, toiled to glorify this remote place and erect a monumental temple to Jupiter upon a tremendous cut stone platform that was already there long before the Roman civilization.

This picture also taken on Zecharia Sitchin's August 1998 exploratory trip to Syria and Lebanon show four tremendous cut stones in one corner of a 2500 foot by 2500 foot platform. Sitchin has identified this pre-diluvian structure as "The Landing Place" described in the Sumerian Epic of Gilgamesh, however, for the purpose of this book it really does not matter what it was used for because there is no Homo sapien on the planet Earth that could cut, lift, transport, and place such one thousand ton stone blocks: that leaves only the Anunnaki.

Mission Control has some of the most compelling Anunnaki evidence as it was built on a massive cut stone platform. It contained several cut stones that weighed 500 to 600 tons each. Sitchin has dated these constructions to approximately 9000 B.C. The man in the above photograph depicts one end of a 500 to 600 ton cut stone in the so called tunnel which is adjacent to the Wailing Wall. Taken on Sitchin's expedition to the Holy Land – September 1997.

Many years later, when Homo sapiens multiplied and inhabited the area it became known as Jerusalem, a focal point of the Jewish, Moslem and Christian religions.

Part Three

Genetics,
Tracing the Origin of Homo Sapiens

Genetics 101

Everyone has known forever that children usually resemble their parents, but it wasn't until the 1950s that just how it happened was being figured out.

A monk, Gregor Mendel, from the Czech Republic had this idea of genetics from his breeding of peas in the monastery garden, in the 1860s. He had the idea that whatever it was that determined the make-up of the future plant or animal came from both parents.

By the early nineteen-hundreds it had been established that the chromosomes played a major role in our genetic make-up, but just how was still a mystery.

The most important strides in clarifying and extending the knowledge of heredity came through the research of Professor Thomas Hunt Morgan and his Columbia University Team, which included Professor H. J. Muller (who, like Professor Morgan, was awarded a Nobel prize). These scientists and others, experimenting with fruit flies, worked out many of the detailed principles and techniques which formed the foundation of the science of modern genetics. Subsequently, geneticists and other scientists from many countries greatly broadened the knowledge and produced many significant new findings directly applicable to human heredity.

The special life substance in genes that endows them with their powers of transmitting hereditary traits has been identified as "DNA" (short for deoxyribonucleic acid). How the DNA worked and the way it sent out its genetic code messages were long a mystery until it was shown in 1953 by two scientists, James Watson and Francis Crick, that the DNA molecule resembled an enormously long, flexible twisted rope ladder (a "double helix"), consisting of two coiled mated stands with rungs in between. The rungs were identified as composed of pairs of chemical bases—adinine (A) joined with thymine (T), or guanine (G), joined with cystosine (C). Formally they are known as nucleotide bases. On any rung either of the pairs could be first or second, so there could be four types of rungs: AT, TA, CG, and GC. With successive rungs (and possibly millions of them in a single DNA molecule) there could be countless arrangements—for example AT, TA, CG, AT, GC, CG, TA, TA, CG, and so on for part of one gene; or CG, TA, CG, CG, AT, AT, CG, GC, TA, etc. for part of other gene. Each sequence carries instructions for guiding the information in cells of one particular protein. The different proteins made by the entire collection of genes in turn direct the carrying out of all the bodies specific processes and functions, from the conception of an individual and on through life.

The foregoing is a greatly simplified summary of the workings of the genetic code, with many technical details omitted. The infinitely varied possibilities in the DNA coding of genes can explain not only the innumerable differences in genetic traits among human beings but the great genetic differences among all the different species of living things, animals and vegetables. All animals and plants like human beings, have DNA as the basic life substance of their chromosomes and genes. The difference between one species and another results from special characteristics and variations in the DNA coding of the genes. Different species also vary in the way their genes are arranged in the chromosomes. For example, compared with the normal human quota of twenty-three pairs of chromosomes, a dog has thirty-nine pairs, a mouse has twenty pairs, a fruit fly has four pairs, a cow has thirty pairs, a gorilla or chimpanzee has twenty-four pairs. Difference in chromosome numbers among species need not be related to an animal's size, and may mean only that the individual chromosomes of one species may carry greater or fewer genes per average chromosome than those of another species. The human quota of chromosomes may carry tens of thousands of genes, and the quota of many other animals may have much the same number. Some of the chromosomes of one species may look almost exactly like those of another species. Taken together, the chromosomes of a human being can be readily distinguished by an expert from those of any other creature though various criteria of size and shape.

The End of Genetics 101

David P. Welden

Mitochondrial DNA (mtDNA)
The Origin of Female *Homo sapiens*

It was discovered that, in addition to the DNA in the cell's nucleus, some DNA exists in the mother's cell but outside the nucleus in bodies called "mitochondria." This DNA does not get mixed with the father's DNA; instead, it is passed on "unadulterated" from mother to daughter to granddaughter, and so on through the generations. This discovery, by Douglas Wallace of Emory University in the 1980s, led him to compare this mtDNA of about 800 women. The surprising conclusion, which he announced at a scientific conference in July 1986, was that the mtDNA in all of them appeared to be so similar that these women must have all descended from a single female ancestor.

The research was picked up by Westly Brown of the University of Michigan, who suggested that by determining the rate of natural mutation of mtDNA, the length of time that had passed since this common ancestor was alive could be calculated. Comparing the mtDNA of twenty-one women from diverse geographical and racial backgrounds, he came to the conclusion that they owed their origin to "a single Mitochondrial Eve" who had lived in Africa between 300,000 and 180,000 years ago.

These intriguing findings were taken up by others, who set out to search for "Eve." Prominent among them was Rebecca Cann of the University of California at Berkeley (later at Hawaii University). Obtaining the placentas of 147 women of different races and geographical backgrounds who gave birth at San Francisco hospitals, she extracted and compared their mtDNA. The conclusion was that they all had a common female ancestor who lived between 300,000 and 150,000 years ago (depending on whether the rate of mutation was two percent or four percent per million years). "We usually assume 250,000 years," Cann stated.

To further test what has come to be called the "Eve Hypothesis," Cann and her colleagues, Allen Wilson and Mark Stoneking, proceeded to examine placentas of about 150 women in America whose ancestors came from Europe, Africa, the Middle East, and Asia, as well placentas from aborigine women in Australia and New Guinea. The result indicated that the African mtDNA was the oldest and all those different women from various races and most diverse geographical and cultural backgrounds had the same sole female ancestor who had lived in Africa between 290,000 and 140,000 years ago.

The Y Chromosome
The Origin of Male Homo sapiens

There are two different ways to find the origin of modern mankind (*Homo sapiens*). For female *Homo sapiens* it is through mitochrondrial DNA (mtDNA), as shown in the preceding pages. For male *Homo sapiens* it is through the Y chromosome, as I will show in the following pages.

Let me point out the tremendous differences between Homo erectus and modern man (*Homo sapiens*). Homo erectus was a hairy apeman that had been evolving for millions of years with very little change to show for it. *Homo sapiens* came suddenly, almost overnight in evolutionary years. The most evolutionary change was his intelligence, which was by far greater; it gave him the ability to think of new ways to do things. He advanced his technology faster than the Neanderthal, soon driving him to extinction. There is no way *Homo sapiens* could happen by chance.

In the 1990s, using the Y chromosome, Michael Hammer of the University of Arizona proved that male *Homo sapiens* originated in Africa. It had already been proven by mitochondrial DNA that female *Homo sapiens* had come out of Africa.

Peter Underhill and Peter Oefner invented a technique called denaturing high-performance liquid chromatography (DHPLC). This technique enabled them to rapidly find DNA mutations, otherwise known as markers.

The invention proved useful for tracing human migration. Most spontaneous mutations do neither harm nor good but simply accumulate in the genome, one at a time as they are passed from one generation to the next. A mutation shared by everybody, therefore, must have arisen in everybody's common ancestor.

In a *Nature Genetics* article titled "Y Chromosome Sequence and the History of Human Population," Peter Underhill, the author, estimated the date when mankind first started at 40,000 to 140,000 years ago.

The purpose of Part 3 of this book on genetics is not to prove where *Homo sapiens* migrated, but rather to prove that Marker No. 168, which was the turning point from Homo erectus (ape-man) to *Homo sapiens* (modern man), was the result of the Anunnaki's genetic cross breeding between themselves and Homo erectus for the purpose of creating a worker to replace themselves in their mines in Africa.

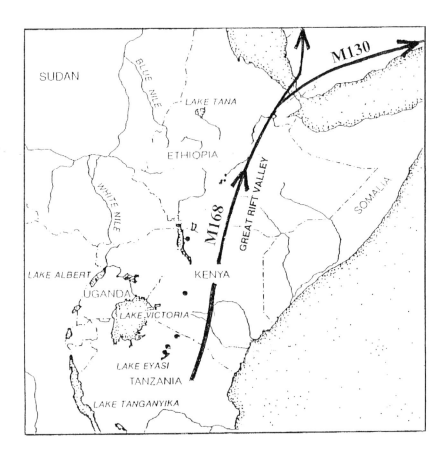

MARKER 168 – THE ORIGIN OF MANKIND

I will admit that there is an apparent discrepancy between the date of the creation of "Adam" and the creation of "Eve." However, I believe if we examine the facts and the assumptions that a conclusion can be reached.

Zecharia Sitchin had been researching and talking about the Anunnaki for years and finally his wife Rena said it's time to quit talking and start writing, which he did.

In 1976 he wrote the *12th Planet*. In this book he stated that 300,000 years ago the Anunnaki created primitive workers through genetic manipulations of themselves and the existing ape-beings "Homo erectus." This proves that the 1976 date of Sitchin's book predates any other researchers that came up with date for the creation of Homo sapiens.

In 1980, Douglas Wallace compared 800 women and came to the conclusion, which he announced at a scientific conference in July 1986, that the mtDNA in all of them appeared to be so similar that these women must have all descended from a single female ancestor.

The approximate figure of 300,000 was reached some time later by four different genetic researchers, namely Westly Brown of the University of Michigan, Rebecca Cann of the University of California at Berkeley (later at Hawaii University), and Allen Wilson and Mark Stoneking.

Now let's look at the apparent discrepancy, which is the difference between 300,000 to 140,000 years ago for mtDNA and 40,000 to 140,000 for the Y chromosome. Of course, if you took the low of the mtDNA of 140,000 and the high of 140,000 for the Y chromosome then there is no discrepancy. However, this is no proof.

Another problem is that Mr. Sitchin says the Adam could not procreate, which was corrected after an unspecified length of time. He says that it was the female "Eve" that was the problem.

Facts and assumptions about the date when Mankind (homo sapiens) first appeared.

Assumption No. 1—Zecharia Sitchin's date of 300,000 years ago is certainly an approximation that he obtained by reading various statements on the clay tablets.

Assumption No. 2—The mtDNA date of 300,000 to 140,000 years ago depends on the rate of mutation and how long after the event (when *Homo sapiens* were created) did the first mutation appear?

Assumption No. 3—The Y chromosome date of 40,000 to 140,000 years ago depends on the rate of mutation of the Y chromosome, and how long after the event did Marker 168 appear?

Fact No. 1—If the two figures between mtDNA and the Y chromosome never jibe, *HOMO SAPIENS* HAPPENED.

Fact No. 2—The odds of *Homo sapiens* just happening are astronomical—IN FACT, IMPOSSIBLE!

Fact No. 3—THE ONLY ANSWER IS SITCHIN'S ANSWER—*HOMO SAPIENS* WERE CREATED BY THE ANUNNAKI, ALIAS NEFILIN!

Part Four

My Conclusions

I was going to make this, Part 4, the all-knowing answer to all of the religions of the world. But the more I thought about it, the more ridiculous it became. So I decided to call it "My Conclusions." Maybe then I could get somebody to agree with me and I wouldn't get in such deep trouble.

Being a somewhat successful inventor and entrepreneur, I sit and think a lot about many things. So I am going to start out with one of the conclusions that I came to while I was sitting and thinking some twenty years ago.

The subject was the birth of Jesus Christ, and I was thinking about the Three Wisemen and how they followed a star from the Orient. And I thought, *you can't follow a star*. This is mainly because the Earth rotates on its axis once every twenty-four hours, and the stars are constantly changing positions; beyond that, you can only see the stars at night.

Columbus was able to navigate to the New World by dead reckoning. This is a process whereby three instruments are required. One is a compass. The second is a rope with knots at measured distances and some kind of object that creates drag when thrown in the water. By counting the knots and estimating the time with the third, an hourglass, they could come up with the knots per hour. Using the compass for their heading they could roughly guess where they were going. This explains why Columbus's destinations ended hundreds of miles apart.

Real accurate navigation—well, fairly accurate navigation—was invented by an Englishman in the fifteenth century. The instruments required were the following: an accurate clock—not a pendulum clock—it had to be able to work on a moving object; a nautical almanac, which gives the positions of major stars for fixed times at Greenwich mean time; and a sextant to measure the angle from the horizon. I am quite sure the Three Wisemen, riding on their camels, didn't have this capability.

Of course, the other solution would be a UFO, and this is my conclusion. Now if this conclusion is correct, this changes something else—that is, he is reported to be a "son of God" with capital G, whereas in actuality he is a son of a god with a small g, which has a connection to the UFO. This is also my conclusion. My third conclusion about this is that Jesus was put here on Earth to teach us how to live, and not to be worshipped.

I am going to restate my system of my conclusion. If my conclusion doesn't make sense to you or even if it does and your present beliefs make more sense to you, then all you have to do is say, "That is not my conclusion."

Does Jesus Christ have supernatural powers, such as his ability to walk on water and have great healing powers? To you and I it seems that way and I believe that these events really happened. However, in many UFO cases, the small aliens with the large black, controlling eyes had the ability to float themselves and Earth humans through closed windows. In fact, in Budd Hopkins's book *Witnessed*, it was actually observed by the two secret servicemen and the U.N. representative. Billy Meier was lifted on board a UFO by some sort of anti-gravity system. So, my conclusion is that Jesus Christ did not have supernatural powers; at least his powers are scientifically possible and are repeated by more scientifically advanced humans and aliens than we humans on Earth.

My next conclusion is the proof that mankind (*Homo sapiens*) was created by a genetic process between the Anunnaki (those who from heaven to Earth came) and Homo erectus (the hairy ape-man).

In the summer of 1994, I was in a bookstore in Des Moines, Iowa, looking for UFO books when I ran across Zecharia Sitchin's book *The 12th Planet*. After reading it, and then some time in the fall of 1994, I wrote Zecharia a letter through his publisher. I had a question. I thought that it seemed unlikely that the orbit time of the Anunnaki's home planet (Nibiru) would just happen to come out as an exact multiple of their numbering system. Their numbering system is based on 6, whereas our numbering system is based on 10. Zecharia wrote and explained that the orbit time of Nibiru wasn't exactly 3600 years, that it could be a few hundred years over or under that figure. He then told me that he and a group of his followers were going on an expedition to Egypt through the Sinai and Jordan and asked me if I wanted to go along. I said yes, and in April 1995, I went with him and the group on the expedition he called "In the footsteps of Moses." After that, which was his third expedition, I went on six more. The last and final of his expeditions was in August 1998. This was mostly through Syria. We made a long one-day trip to Baalbek, Lebanon. Baalbek, Lebanon, is where I took the picture of that 1200-ton cut stone. Now, back to the original trip. We went through the Great Pyramid of Giza, and this totally convinced me that Sitchin was right—the Great Pyramids of Giza were definitely built by the Anunnaki. All of the features of the Great Pyramid as shown in Part 2 were exactly there to be seen; there is no way that the Great Pyramids could have been built by the Pharaohs.

At the end of Part 3, on genetics, I have proof that *Homo sapiens* were created by the Anunnaki. However, there is one other proof the Anunnaki (those who from heaven to earth came) were present on Earth and were responsible for mankind (*Homo sapiens*) and that is on page 314 in the book *Message from the Pleiades*.

Billy Meier says, "That is astonishing! Then the script on Earth was not developed by Earth men themselves?"

Semjase says, "If you speak of the Earthbound forefathers of your human race, and not of the heavenly ancestors, then you are correct. It (the script) was first brought by the Sons of Heaven, who were the ones responsible for the reemergence of the Earth humans from savagery."

Spencer Wells wrote the book *The Journey of Man* (which came out in 2002) in which he did a terrific job of tracking mankind toward its origin by the use of the Y chromosome. The December 2004 *Discover* magazine had on its cover a large Y and announced its feature article: "Secrets of the Y Chromosome by Spencer Wells."

However, tracking mankind *toward its origin* is not the same as tracking it *to its origin*. In his book *The Journey of Man*, and on page 83 and 84, he makes an attempt to track mankind *to its origin*.

The following is my summation of what he wrote, without infringing on his copyright and not being transformative.

In those days in Africa where Homo sapiens first appeared, Homo erectus (the hairy ape-man, who had changed very little in several million years) traveled around in small groups called clans. He proposed a hypothetical situation where one of the clan families has a male son who is much different from all the others. He learned to speak at a much younger age and he was innovative. In other words, he could make things better than any of the other children.

As he grew up he was taught the ape-man trades, such as hunting and making simple tools. His skills soon surpassed all the other clansmen and at an early age he became the clan leader. Because of his advanced skills and knowledge the clan grew and became more competitive with other clans. The children he fathered were also more advanced.

In other words, he is saying that suddenly from one generation to another the hairy ape-man became *Homo sapiens*.

This is where my next my conclusion starts!

This story by Spencer Wells is impossible, and I am sure he knows it. There are simply too many differences to have it happen like that. The only way it could happen is to have some beings with superior knowledge make genetic changes.

And so, Zecharia Sitchin's story of how it happened is absolutely credible, and it is backed up by the Pleiadians.

My next conclusion is a direct quote on page 189 and 190 in the book *Message from the Pleiades* by Semjase and Billy Meier.

Semjase: Before today we were discussing other things, but today I want to continue with the discussion of spirit. A person may react to the word or the designation "the Creation" in different ways, as though it were something apart and beautiful and good. Such is not exactly the case. Such characterizations as "omnipresent," "all powerful," and "all knowing" are valid characterizations of the nature of the Creation. Millions of religious humans do not understand the true nature of the Creation. Whenever they speak of it, they tend to personify it as a God-like being (which is then itself a separation from the Creation), and they confuse the idea of the Creation. So it is very important to know as much as possible about the character and the nature of the Creation, for when the word is understood properly it buoys the inner mind and connects it to its source as soon as the word is heard.

The experience reveals the Creation as unlimited beauty, harmony, knowledge, and truth...enduring endlessly. So whenever a human perceives a thing of beauty—a flower, an animal, clouds, water, landscape, music, color, etc.—he considers it in connection with the limitless grandeur of the Creation itself. When a human recognizes and realizes this, then he knows that this recognition springs from limitness cognition. Even inside the tiniest creature, like a microbe, he sees the limitless Creation.

The Creation is inside of every human being (and every other Creation and thing), being a fraction of that manifestation itself. Once this thought has penetrated deeply inside a person and he can experience it, he loses all fear and doubt. When he knows his contact is with knowing, almighty Creation, he can enjoy peace and tranquility. Reflection on this gives the name "Creation" a great meaning. The more he meditates on this reality, the more his intelligence is illuminated, and the more powerful his personality becomes. His whole life and labor is blessed. The Creation rises in his consciousness and he senses peace, strength, knowledge, and wisdom, delight, and hope. He can overcome obstacles and achieve his objectives, and he suddenly has no more need for purely material things. One must learn a spiritual-intellectual manner of thinking and recognize its validity until the first successes are achieved.

But the way does not stop here, because further exploration, research, development, and recognition lead to limitless endurance of time. Everything may happen in the course of time to prevent one from achieving his objectives, but the spiritualized person knows no limit and does not allow himself to be stopped short of his goals of any events of the future. For him the future always exists in the present, where he becomes determined to do everything here and now to obtain the highest spiritual state of consciousness. He does not fear the future for the future is now, just as present as the present itself.

When the spiritualized being sees others before him, he sees the Creation in them.

Meier:	What you are saying sounds so understandable and logical. If only humans could comprehend it.
Semjase:	So they will, but this will not happen tomorrow. You and your group are only laying the basic stones for an avalanche, which will start much later.